CONTEMPORARY'S
Working in English

WITHDRAWN

CONTEMPORARY'S
Working in English
Beginning Language Skills for the World of Work
BOOK 2

Marianne Brems

Senior Editor
Julie Landau

Consultants
Fiona Armstrong
New York City Board of Education

Kathleen Santopietro
Consultant, Teacher Training
Colorado Department of Education

Catherine Porter
Consultant
Illinois ESL Adult Education Service Center

CB
CONTEMPORARY BOOKS
a division of NTC/CONTEMPORARY PUBLISHING GROUP
Lincolnwood, Illinois USA

CARVER COUNTY LIBRARY SYSTEM

Library of Congress Cataloging-in-Publication Data

Brems, Marianne.
    Working in English 2 : beginning language skills for the world of
work / Marianne Brems.
       p.   cm.
   ISBN 0-8092-4169-2
   1. English language—Textbooks for foreign speakers.   2. English
language—Business English.   3. Readers—Work.   4. Work.   I. Title
II. Title: Working in English two.
PE1128.B673   1990
428.2'4'02465—dc20   90-2428
                                                                       CIP

Special thanks to Central Baptist Home of Norridge, Illinois,
Metraflex of Chicago, and Edward Rozalewicz.

ISBN: 0-8092-4169-2

Published by Contemporary Books,
a division of NTC/Contemporary Publishing Group, Inc.,
4255 West Touhy Avenue,
Lincolnwood (Chicago), Illinois 60646-1975 U.S.A.
© 1991 by Marianne Brems
All rights reserved. No part of this book may be reproduced,
stored in a retrieval system, or transmitted in any form or by any means,
electronic, mechanical, photocopying, recording, or otherwise,
without prior permission of the publisher.
Manufactured in the United States of America.

9 0 C(K) 15 14 13 12

Editorial Director Caren Van Slyke	*Cover Design* Lois Koehler
Editorial Craig Bolt Joan Conover Kathy Osmus Charlotte Ullman Lisa Dillman Ana Flanagan Laura Larson Betsy Rubin Sally Wigginton	*Illustrator* Guy Wolek *Photography* Ralph J. Brunke *Art & Production* Ophelia M. Chambliss-Jones Rosemary Morrissey-Herzberg Sue Springston
Editorial Production Manager Norma Fioretti	*Typography* Ellen M. Yukel
Production Editors Jean Farley Brown Pam Richardson	Cover photo © by Michael Slaughter
Production Assistant Marina Micari	

Contents

To the Instructor vi

FINDING A JOB

1. Personal Information 2
2. Occupations and Skills 14
3. Finding Jobs 26
4. The Interview 38
5. Pay and Benefits 50

KEEPING A JOB

6. Talking with Coworkers 62
7. Asking Questions at Work 74
8. Reporting Absence 86
9. Following Instructions 98
10. Asking for Help 110
11. Apologizing 122
12. Requesting Location 134
13. Observing Safety 146
14. Work Schedule Changes 158
15. Asking for a Promotion 170

To the Instructor

Overview of the Series

Contemporary's *Working in English* series is designed to help you teach your beginning ESL students how to communicate and function effectively in the world of work. Throughout these books, students learn and use language they need to get and keep a job, as well as explore cultural issues relevant to the workplace. Problem solving and decision making, skills needed by all employees at every level, are practiced as well. *Working in English* is appropriate for:

- regular ESL classrooms,
- pre-employment and general VESL classes, and
- workplace literacy programs.

The program is comprised of these four books:

Book 1: A Picture-Based Approach for the World of Work (level: low beginning)
Book 1: Teacher's Guide
Book 2: Beginning Language Skills for the World of Work (level: high beginning)
Book 2: Teacher's Guide

Each teacher's guide provides detailed, step-by-step teaching suggestions for each page, along with extension activities and tips for new teachers.

Book 2: Instructional Design

While each chapter is uniquely structured to meet the demands of the competency, certain features recur throughout the book. A brief explanation follows.

Dialogues present language for real-life workplace situations and introduce the competency for each chapter. Dialogues are usually followed by:

- Check Your Understanding (monitors students' comprehension of key concepts and language) and
- Practice (helps reinforce the competency students have learned).

The **Vocabulary** page presents visuals that can be used to pre-teach words in the dialogue. Also, after the vocabulary exercise is completed, this page becomes a mini-dictionary for the chapter.

Talking Together encompasses a variety of activities that emphasize interaction and meaningful communication. Samples include pair work, discussion questions, and role plays.

Words for Work is a print-based vocabulary exercise in which students practice key words from the chapter.

Speaking Practice focuses on speaking and listening skills useful in the workplace. Speaking Practice activities provide opportunities for pair and small group work. Information gaps, charts, and other communicative activities are highlighted.

Structure Work presents grammar in a context that will aid students in successful on-the-job communication. Depending on their level, your students may need grammar instruction beyond what is presented in this text before they complete the Structure Work.

Problem Solving helps students hone their skills in decision making and problem solving. This feature also addresses issues of appropriate behavior in the American workplace.

More detailed suggestions for using this book can be found in Contemporary's *Working in English, Book 2: Teacher's Guide.*

Chapter 1
Personal Information

HOW ARE YOU?

Look and Listen

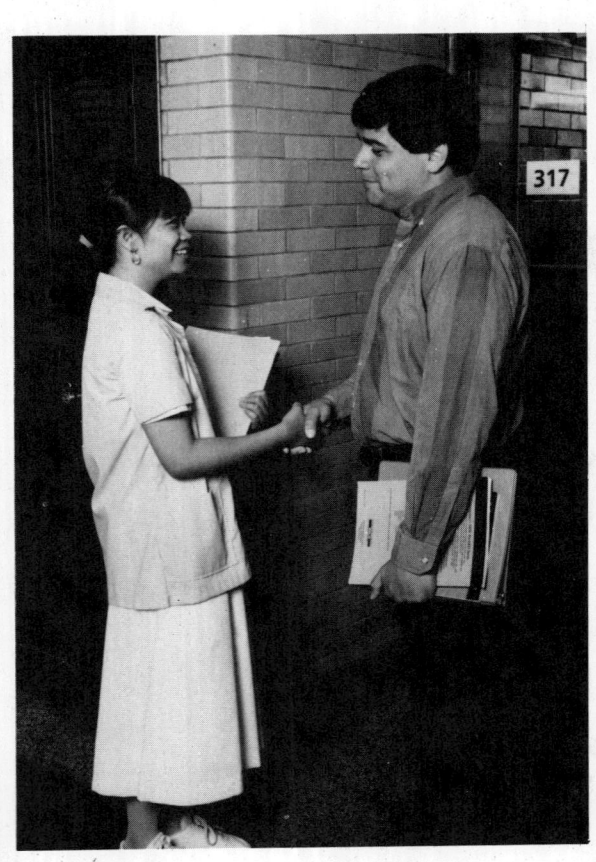

Mei: Hi, how are you? My name's Mei.
Juan: Hi, I'm Juan. Nice to meet you.
Mei: Are you a new student?
Juan: Yes, I am.
Mei: Where are you from?
Juan: El Salvador. And you?
Mei: I'm from Viet Nam.
Juan: Are you working now?
Mei: Yes. I'm a nurse's aide. And you?
Juan: I work in a factory.

Check Your Understanding

Circle Yes or No. Follow the example.

1. Mei is a student. (Yes) No
2. Juan is a student. Yes No
3. Juan is from Mexico. Yes No
4. Mei is from El Salvador. Yes No
5. Juan is a factory worker. Yes No
6. Juan and Mei are old friends. Yes No

Practice

Practice the conversation. Then answer the questions.

Mei: Where do you work?
Pedro: I'm not working now.
Mei: Excuse me. Could you repeat that?
Pedro: I'm not working now. I don't have a job.

1. Is Pedro working now?
2. Does Mei understand Pedro? What does she say?
3. Are you working now?

Teacher's Note: More detailed suggestions for using this book can be found in Contemporary's *Working in English, Book 2: Teacher's Guide.*

WHERE DO YOU WORK?

Look and Listen

Juan: Hi, Mei. How's it going?

Mei: I'm tired. I just got off work.

Juan: Where do you work?

Mei: At Midland Hospital.

Juan: That's far away.

Mei: Yes—about an hour by bus.

Juan: Do you like your job?

Mei: The work is OK, but the pay is low.

Check Your Understanding

Circle the correct answer.

1. Where are Mei and Juan?   hospital   school
2. How does Mei feel?   tired   happy
3. Where does Mei work?   hospital   restaurant
4. Is it close to school or far away?   close   far
5. Is the pay high or low?   high   low

Practice

Fill out the first row of the chart for yourself. Then interview four classmates.

Name	Are you working now?	Where do you work?	What's your job?

VOCABULARY

Circle the best word for each picture. Then write it in the blank to the right. Follow the example.

1. groundskeeper   cook
   mechanic
   (cook)

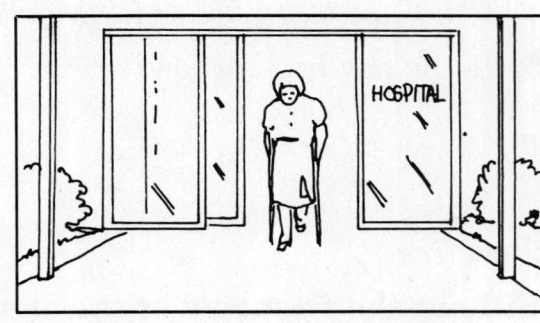

4. hospital
   restaurant
   nurse's aide

2. mechanic
   nurse's aide
   groundskeeper

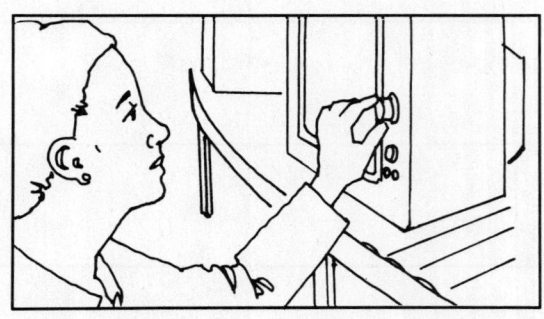

5. factory worker
   cook
   nurse's aide

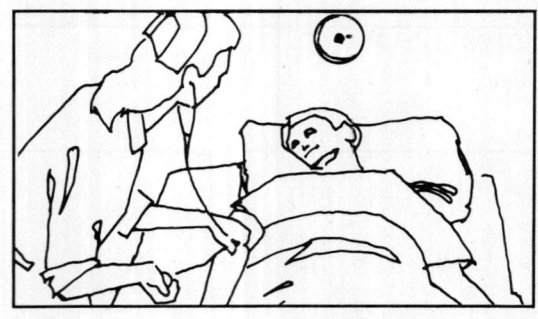

3. cook
   groundskeeper
   nurse's aide

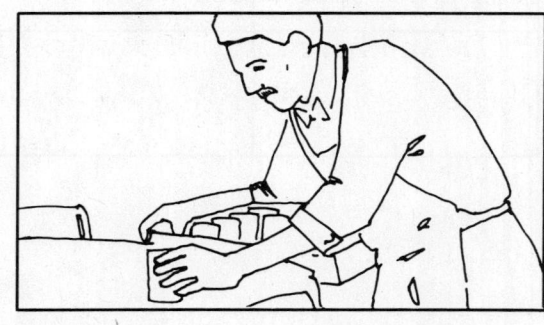

6. cook
   hospital
   restaurant

TALKING TOGETHER

My name is Marco.
I'm a cook.
I work at Rosa's Restaurant.
I speak Spanish at work.
I read orders in Spanish.
The customers speak English.
I understand a little.

Part 1

Answer the questions.

1. Where does Marco work?
2. What is his job?
3. Does he speak English at work?
4. Does he hear English at work?
5. Does he read or write English at work?

Part 2

Ask a partner these questions.

1. Do you hear English at work? What do you hear?
2. Do you speak English at work? What do you say?
3. Do you read English at work? What do you read?
4. Do you write English at work? What do you write?
5. How can you learn more English at work?
6. Is it important to speak English at work? Why or why not?

WORDS FOR WORK

Part 1

Write each of the following words in the correct list. Follow the example.

work	nurse's aide	restaurant
~~groundskeeper~~	mechanic	repeat
look	hospital	speak
write	hear	

Jobs 　　　　　　　Workplaces 　　　　　　　Action Words

groundskeeper 　　_____ 　　_____

_____ 　　　_____ 　　_____

_____ 　　　_____ 　　_____

　　　　　　　　　　　　　　　　　　　_____

　　　　　　　　　　　　　　　　　　　_____

Part 2

Which word does *not* belong? Cross out the word. Follow the example.

1. restaurant   hospital   ~~job~~   school
2. El Salvador   restaurant   Mexico   China
3. job   write   speak   meet
4. groundskeeper   work   cook   nurse's aide
5. mechanic   repeat   groundskeeper   nurse's aide

PARTNER WORK

Person 1

Speak to a partner. Start with a, b, or c in number 1. Your partner will choose a response. Your partner's part is on page 10.

1. a. Hi, how are you? My name is Juan.
   b. Do you speak English at work?
   c. How's your job?

2. a. That's great! Who do you talk to?
   b. Nice to meet you, too. Where are you from?
   c. Where do you work?

3. a. What's your job?
   b. I'm from El Salvador.
   c. Lucky you. I only speak Korean at work.

4. a. I work at the tire factory.
   b. San Salvador. What about you?
   c. No.

nine 9

PARTNER WORK

Person 2

Your partner will speak to you. Answer with a, b, or c in number 1. Your partner's part is on page 9.

1. **a.** All the time.
   b. Nice to meet you, Juan. My name is Zosia.
   c. It's OK, but the pay is low.

2. **a.** I'm from Poland. And you?
   b. I talk to the customers.
   c. At the Gold Star Restaurant.

3. **a.** I'm a busboy. What about you?
   b. Do you have American friends?
   c. That's a beautiful country. What city are you from?

4. **a.** Really? My brother works at that factory, too.
   b. I'm from Warsaw.
   c. You need to meet more people!

STRUCTURE WORK

Review the verb *to be*.

I	am	we	are
you	are	you	are
he			
she	is	they	are
it			

Complete each question and answer with *is*, *are*, or *am*. Follow the example.

1. How __are__ you?

    I __am__ fine.

2. Where _____ Mei from?

    She _____ from Viet Nam.

3. What _____ Juan's job?

    He _____ a factory worker.

4. _____ Mei and Juan students?

    Yes, they _____.

5. Where _____ Pedro from?

    He _____ from Peru.

6. Where _____ you from?

    I _____ from Haiti.

7. What _____ Mei's job?

    She _____ a nurse's aide.

8. Where _____ the hospital?

    It _____ far away.

9. _____ Mei happy with her job?

    No, she _____ not.

10. _____ you happy with your job?

    Yes, I _____.

PROBLEM SOLVING

It's a Pleasure to Meet You

Listen and answer the questions.

Mei: Hello, Pedro. This is my husband, John.

Pedro: It's a pleasure to meet you, Don.

John: Nice to meet you, too. By the way, my name is John.

Pedro: I'm sorry, John. Please excuse me.

John: No problem.

1. What mistake does Pedro make?
2. Does John know Pedro made a mistake?
3. How do you think Pedro feels?
4. Have you ever made a mistake like this? What happened? How did you feel?

I Don't Understand

Look at the pictures. Then answer the questions.

1. What do you say to your friends when you don't understand?
2. What do you say to your teacher when you don't understand?
3. What can you do when you don't understand your boss?

Chapter 2
Occupations and Skills

I'M A CARPENTER

Look and Read

My name is Mikyung Park.
I'm a seamstress.
I sew seams and mend clothes.

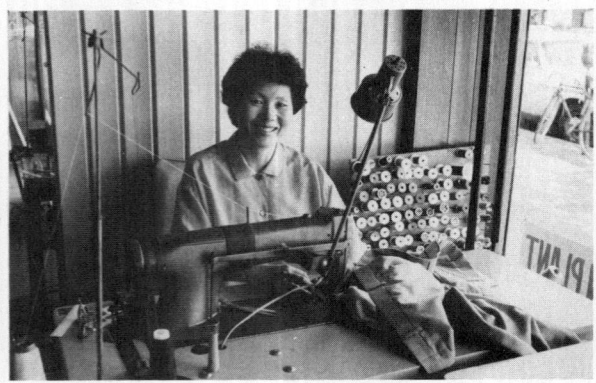

My name is Jean Baptiste.
I'm a painter.
I paint houses and signs.

My name is Charles Wilson.
I'm a carpenter.
I build houses.

My name is _____.
I'm a _____.
I _____.

Check Your Understanding

Circle Yes or No.

1. Is he a groundskeeper?
   Yes   No

2. Is she a painter?
   Yes   No

3. Is he a carpenter?
   Yes   No

4. Is she a seamstress?
   Yes   No

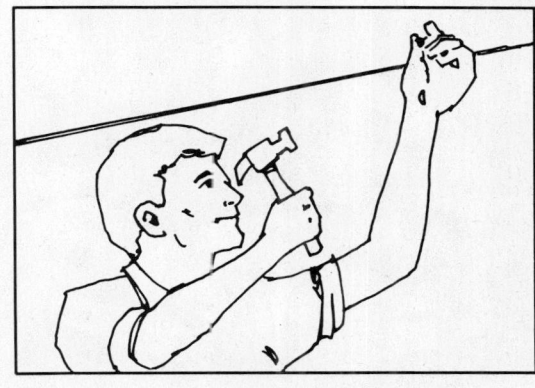

5. Is he a mechanic?
   Yes   No

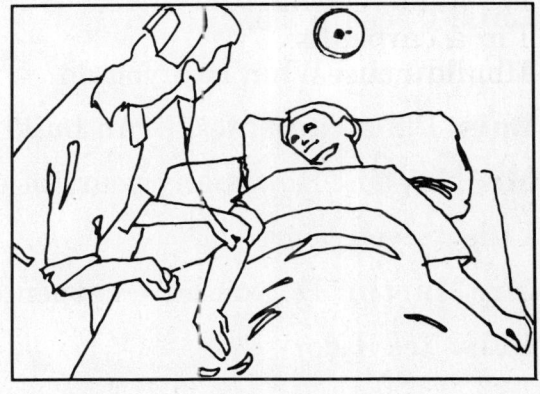

6. Is she a cook?
   Yes   No

I NEED A JOB

Look and Listen

Luis: I need a job.
Mr. Martin: What can you do?
Luis: I'm a carpenter. I can build houses.
Mr. Martin: How many years of experience do you have?
Luis: Seven years.
Mr. Martin: Do you have carpenter's tools?
Luis: Yes, I do.

Check Your Understanding

Answer the questions.

1. Is Mr. Martin a job counselor?
2. Does Luis have a job now?
3. Does Luis have tools?
4. Can Luis build houses?
5. Does he have eight or seven years of experience?

Practice

Write in the information. Then practice asking and answering the questions with a partner.

1. What can you do?

   I can _____.

2. What's your job?

   I'm a _____.

3. How many years of experience do you have?

   _____ years.

4. What tools or equipment do you use in your work?

   I use _____.

VOCABULARY

1. taxi driver

4. hairdresser
   barber

2. housekeeper

5. stock clerk

3. parking attendant

6. waitress
   waiter

Match each job to the appropriate duty. Work with a partner.

____ cleans houses   ____ serves food

____ drives passengers   ____ stocks shelves

____ cuts hair   ____ parks cars

TALKING TOGETHER

Think of two jobs you have had. Draw a picture of what you did and write down your duties. Then tell a partner about your jobs. Follow the example.

Example:

Job: Taxi driver
Duties: Drive taxi
Talk to passengers
Take money

Your Jobs

Job: _____
Duties: _____
_____
_____
_____

Job: _____
Duties: _____
_____
_____
_____

nineteen 19

WORDS FOR WORK

Part 1

Find each hidden word and circle it. Then cross off the word on the list. Follow the examples.

X	C	B	U	I	L	D	S	M	Z
R	L	C	U	T	T	R	T	A	F
S	E	R	V	E	A	I	O	K	W
T	A	F	I	X	L	V	C	E	O
Y	N	P	A	R	K	E	K	P	R
P	A	I	N	T	N	E	E	D	K

~~BUILD~~
~~DRIVE~~
PARK
TALK
CLEAN
SERVE
CUT
FIX
PAINT
NEED
MAKE
WORK
STOCK

Part 2

Write the name of a job in the blank. Follow the example.

1. He parks cars. He's a *parking attendant*.
2. She cuts hair. She's a _____.
3. He drives passengers. He's a _____.
4. She serves food. She's a _____.
5. He stocks shelves. He's a _____.
6. She cleans houses. She's a _____.

ASK ABOUT IT

Practice the conversation.

○ What's your name?
● Luis Ortega.
○ What's your job?
● I'm a carpenter.
○ What do you do?
● I build houses.

Interview five classmates. Fill in the spaces below. If you don't have a job, list things you can do or like to do.

Name	Job	Duties
Luis Ortega	carpenter	build houses

twenty-one 21

USING SKILLS AT HOME

When you work at home, you use many skills. Read each skill and put a check (✓) in the first column if you use that skill at home. Put a check (✓) in the second column if you like to use that skill.

Skill	Use at home	Enjoy
clean houses		
sew clothes		
plant flowers		
fix cars		
fix sinks		
sell things		
have parties		
meet new people		
care for children		
cut hair		
cook food		
serve food		
paint houses		
go shopping		
drive cars		

STRUCTURE WORK

Make ten sentences from the words below. For each sentence, use one word from Group A, Group B, and Group C. You may use some of the words in Group B or C twice. Begin each sentence with a word from Group A. Remember to put an *s* or an *es* on the action word. Follow the example.

Group A	Group B	Group C
salesclerk	clean	cars
housekeeper	stock	trees
mechanic	park	hair
taxi driver	talk to	passengers
hairdresser	paint	a taxi
groundskeeper	fix	shelves
stock clerk	drive	houses
painter	cut	offices
carpenter	trim	customers
parking attendant	build	
	plant	

1. A salesclerk talks to customers.
2.
3.
4.
5.
6.
7.
8.
9.
10.

twenty-three 23

PROBLEM SOLVING

Skills and Jobs

Read each question below. Choose the answers from the jobs in the list. List all answers you think are correct. Follow the example.

	Jobs	
groundskeeper	mechanic	carpenter
bus driver	waiter/waitress	housekeeper
taxi driver	stock clerk	painter
parking attendant	salesclerk	barber/hairdresser

1. Who cleans?

    housekeeper
    groundskeeper

2. Who deals with people?

3. Who takes money from customers?

4. Who needs tools?

5. Who does a service?

6. Who needs to drive well?

7. Who organizes?

8. Who needs to dress neatly?

Your Skills

1. Look at pages 19 and 22. What are your skills? Copy them here.

   _____   _____   _____

   _____   _____   _____

   _____   _____   _____

2. Which skills do you like best? Number the list above from what you like most to what you like least. Put *1* next to the skill you like most.

3. Rewrite the list in order.

   1. _____
   2. _____
   3. _____
   4. _____
   5. _____
   6. _____
   7. _____
   8. _____
   9. _____

4. Look at the first three skills on your list. Write the names of three jobs that use those skills. Work with a group.

   1. _____
   2. _____
   3. _____

twenty-five 25

Chapter 3
Finding Jobs

I WANT TO WORK IN DAYCARE

Look and Listen

Job Opening
Daycare worker
wanted.
Experience
preferred.
Part-time,
9 A.M. to 3 P.M.
Starting pay:
$5 an hour.
Apply at:
Walton Daycare
Center
248 Lindell Street.

Veena: I need a part-time job. I'd like to work in daycare.

Mr. Martin: Do you have experience?

Veena: Yes. I have two years' experience.

Mr. Martin: Here's an opening for a daycare worker.

Veena: What is the pay?

Mr. Martin: Five dollars an hour.

Veena: I'd like to apply.

Mr. Martin: OK. But you have to apply in person.

Veena: I'm sorry. I don't understand.

Mr. Martin: You have to go to the daycare center. Here's the address.

Check Your Understanding

Answer the questions.

1. Where is Veena?
2. What does Veena need?
3. What kind of job is open?
4. Is the job full-time or part-time?
5. Is the pay $6 or $5 an hour?
6. What are the hours?
7. Does Veena have experience?
8. Where does Veena have to go to apply for the job?

Practice

1. What if you don't have experience for a job? You may still have the skills. Read the conversation below.

    You: I'd like to work in daycare.

    Job Counselor: Do you have experience?

    You: No, but <u>I have children.</u>
                  I love to play with children.
                  I baby-sit a lot.
                  I take care of my sister's children.

2. Think of a job you want to do. Practice the conversation above stating skills that you have for that job.

CAN YOU COME FOR AN INTERVIEW?

Look and Listen

Mrs. Johnson: Hello. May I help you?

Veena: Yes. I'm here to apply for the daycare job.

Mrs. Johnson: Do you have experience taking care of children?

Veena: Yes, I do. Two years' experience.

Mrs. Johnson: Can you come for an interview at 3:00 tomorrow?

Veena: No, but I can come at 4:00.

Mrs. Johnson: OK. See you then.

Practice

Practice the dialogue. Then substitute the words below each picture for the underlined words.

○ I'm here to apply for the <u>taxi driver</u> job.
● Do you have experience <u>driving a taxi</u>?
○ Yes, I do.

1. taxi driver
driving a taxi

4. painter
painting signs

2. food-service worker
serving food

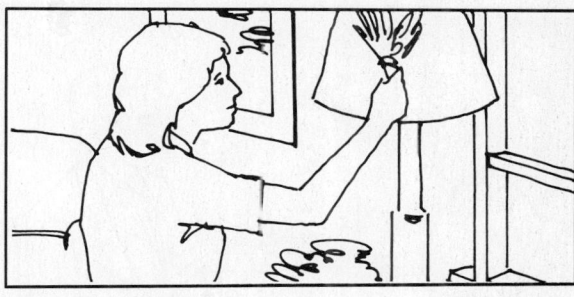

5. housecleaner
cleaning houses

3. hairdresser
cutting hair

6. mechanic
fixing cars

What other skills and personal qualities are needed for these jobs?

VOCABULARY

> friends   newspaper ads
> Help Wanted signs   job counselor

Answer the questions.

1. Where are these people looking for jobs? Match each word or phrase to the correct picture.
2. How did you get your job?

TALKING TOGETHER

Part 1

Interview your classmates. Ask how they got their jobs.

How did you get your job?	Names
I saw a job counselor.	
I asked friends.	
I read a HELP WANTED sign.	
I read newspaper ads.	

Part 2

Think about what you want in a job and answer these questions.

1. Do you want to work days or nights?
2. Do you want to work alone or with other people?
3. Do you want to work full-time or part-time?
4. Do you want to work indoors or outdoors?
5. Do you want to do something physical, like work in a warehouse or clean houses?
6. Do you want to do something that is not so physical, like being a cashier or working in an office?
7. Do you want a job in which you can wear casual clothes, a uniform, or more formal clothes?
8. Do you have things to do, like take care of a child or work another job, that affect the hours you can work?

SPEAKING PRACTICE

Pao needs a new job. He works as a gas station attendant, but he wants to get a job as a mechanic. Where should he look for a job?

Ways of Finding a Job	Advantages (+)	Disadvantages (−)
Newspaper ads		
Friends		
Help Wanted signs		
Job counselor		

Practice

1. Work with a group. Think of one reason *for* using each way of finding work and one reason *against*.
2. Think about the jobs you want. Think of one reason for using each method of job hunting and one against.

SETTING UP AN INTERVIEW

Sometimes you need to call to set up a job interview. Practice the following conversation. Then, with a partner, repeat the call using your own information in place of the underlined words.

Employee: Billy's Restaurant.

Veena: Hello. This is <u>Veena Patel</u>. I'm calling about the opening for a <u>cashier</u>.

Employee: Just a minute, please.

Manager: This is the manager speaking.

Veena: Hello. This is <u>Veena Patel</u>. I'm calling about the opening for a <u>cashier</u>.

Manager: Can you come in for an interview at <u>9:00 tomorrow</u>?

Veena: At <u>9:00 tomorrow</u>? Yes, I can.

Manager: Good. See you then.

WORDS FOR WORK

pay	Monday	
hours	Tuesday	
interview	Wednesday	weekdays
application	Thursday	
job opening	Friday	
in person	Saturday	weekend
personnel manager	Sunday	
company	today	
	tomorrow	

Practice

Listen to the questions and write some of your own. Think of answers. Then practice with a partner.

Questions to ask an interviewer:

1. Is the job available?
2. Can you tell me more about the job?
3. Can I come in after work tomorrow?
4. What are the hours?
5. What's the pay?
6. What's the address of the company?

Questions you want to ask:

_____
_____
_____
_____
_____
_____

STRUCTURE WORK

Present Tense and Present Continuous Tense

The present tense is used for actions that happen regularly.
For example:
> She **drives** a school bus every morning.

The action takes place regularly—every morning—so you use the present tense.

The present continuous tense is used for actions that are taking place right now. For example:
> She **is driving** a school bus right now.

Practice

Choose the present or the present continuous (–*ing*) form of the verb from the list below.

need	serve	go	look	buy
tell	clean	sell	fix	read

1. Miriam _goes_ to a job counselor every week.
2. Oscar needs a job. He _____ a newspaper every morning at the grocery store.
3. Right now, Victor's friend _____ him about a job where he works.
4. Helen _____ the offices every Wednesday.
5. Stanley is a food-service worker. He _____ food in the cafeteria.
6. Hugo _____ at a HELP WANTED sign in the window at Fast Gas service station.
7. Rona _____ clothing every Saturday and Sunday from 12 P.M. to 5 P.M.
8. Matilda _____ a job.
9. She _____ every HELP WANTED sign she sees.
10. Henry _____ Mr. Ching's car right now.

PROBLEM SOLVING

Part 1

Read the job descriptions. Then answer the questions.

1.
> Groundskeeper.
> Full-time.
> Experience
> preferred.
> Must have
> driver's license.

2.
> Mechanic at
> Fast Gas
> Service Station.
> Work weekends,
> part-time.
> Must have
> experience.

3.
> School Bus
> Driver.
> 20-30 hrs./wk.
> No nights
> or weekends.
> Good driver.
> Good pay.

4.
> Sales Clerk
> for large
> department
> store. Must
> have neat
> appearance and
> like people.
> Full-time.

5.
> Housecleaner
> with
> experience.
> Must have own
> transportation.
> Must be
> reliable and
> work hard.
> Starting pay
> $8 hr.

1. Which jobs are full-time?
2. Which jobs require experience?
3. Which jobs require a driver's license?
4. Which job requires weekend work?
5. Which jobs would you want? Why?

Part 2

Work with two or three other students. Match each applicant with the best job or jobs on page 36. Write the number of the job next to the description. Sometimes there is more than one answer.

Applicants

____ • Martha likes to work outdoors.
• She goes to school at night.
• She likes people.

____ • Oscar likes to fix all kinds of cars.
• He is a good driver.
• He needs a weekend job.

____ • Matilde is a single parent.
• She doesn't speak much English.
• She keeps her apartment very clean.

____ • Pierre likes to dress well and look good.
• He likes to work indoors.
• He wants to make good money.

____ • Miriam wants to come home from work by 4:00.
• She doesn't want to work full-time.
• She has a driver's license.

About You

What is most important to *you* about a job? Number the choices in order of importance. If you like, write a new choice in the blank.

____ good pay

____ good hours

____ kind of work I enjoy

____ good boss

____ good location

____ _____

Why?

Chapter 4
The Interview

HOW LONG HAVE YOU BEEN AT YOUR JOB?

Look and Listen

Job Opening
Warehouse worker needed to do shipping, receiving, and stocking. Good driving record. Experience required.

Mr. Sanchez: Daniel, tell me a little about your work experience. Are you working now?

Daniel: Yes, I am. I work in a warehouse.

Mr. Sanchez: What do you do?

Daniel: I operate a forklift.

Mr. Sanchez: That's good. How long have you been at your job?

Daniel: A year and a half.

Check Your Understanding

Circle Yes or No.

1. Daniel is a warehouse worker.   Yes   No
2. He has a job now.   Yes   No
3. He serves customers.   Yes   No
4. He can use a forklift.   Yes   No
5. He has worked in the warehouse for 18 months.   Yes   No
6. The interviewer likes Daniel's work experience.   Yes   No

Practice

Answer these questions. Then interview three classmates and complete the chart.

1. How long have you been living in the United States?
2. How long have you been living in your city?
3. How long have you been taking English classes?
4. How long have you been at your job?

Name	Living in the U.S.	Living in your city	Taking English classes	At your job
Daniel Gomez	5 years	3 years	4 months	1½ years

CAN YOU TAKE INVENTORY?

Look and Listen

Mr. Sanchez: How much education do you have?

Daniel: I finished eighth grade in Mexico. I'm taking English classes now.

Mr. Sanchez: Can you take inventory?

Daniel: I'm sure I can learn.

Mr. Sanchez: Do you know how to do shipping and receiving?

Daniel: Yes, I do that now. I have a year and a half of experience.

Mr. Sanchez: When can you start work?

Daniel: Next week.

Mr. Sanchez: OK, Daniel. Is there anything else you want to say?

Daniel: I'm a hard worker. I'm very responsible, too.

Practice

Part 1

Answer the questions.

1. How much education do you have?
2. Name three of your personal qualities.
3. How much experience do you have at your job?
4. When can you start work?

Part 2

Interview three classmates. Follow the example.

Name	Education	Personal Qualities
Daniel Gomez	8th grade, English classes	1. hard worker 2. responsible 3. organized
		1. 2. 3.
		1. 2. 3.
		1. 2. 3.

VOCABULARY

Look at each picture and decide if it is an example of *education*, *work experience*, or *work attitude*. Write your answer in the blank. Work with another student. Sometimes there is more than one possible answer.

1. Duc was a mechanic for a year and a half.

4. Anne comes to work late every day.

2. Dongsheng studied at a university in China.

5. Evelyn has been a parking attendant for one year.

3. Mei is learning English at the Adult Learning Center.

6. Simon is friendly to customers.

TALKING TOGETHER

Marie is interviewing for a job as a seamstress.

Interviewer: Can you tell me a little about your experience at your last job?
Marie: I'm sorry. I don't understand.
Interviewer: What did you do at your last job?
Marie: I worked in a laundry.
Interviewer: For how long?
Marie: Three years.
Interviewer: Are you married?
Marie: I'm sorry. I'd rather not answer that.

Practice

1. What job does Marie want?
2. What questions does the interviewer ask?
3. The interviewer asks Marie, "Are you married?" What does Marie say?
4. It is against the law for interviewers to ask personal questions. What are personal questions?
5. If an interviewer asks you a personal question, what can you say?

SPEAKING PRACTICE

Graciela is going to a job interview. She calls to ask for directions. Look at the map and follow the directions. Then draw the route that Graciela should take.

Graciela: How do I get to the company?

Receptionist: Get off the number 42 bus at Third Avenue and R Street. Go two blocks east on Third Avenue. Turn left on T Street and go two blocks north.

Graciela: Two blocks east on Third Avenue, left on T Street, and two blocks north.

Receptionist: Yes. Our company is on the corner of First Avenue and T Street.

Graciela: Thank you very much.

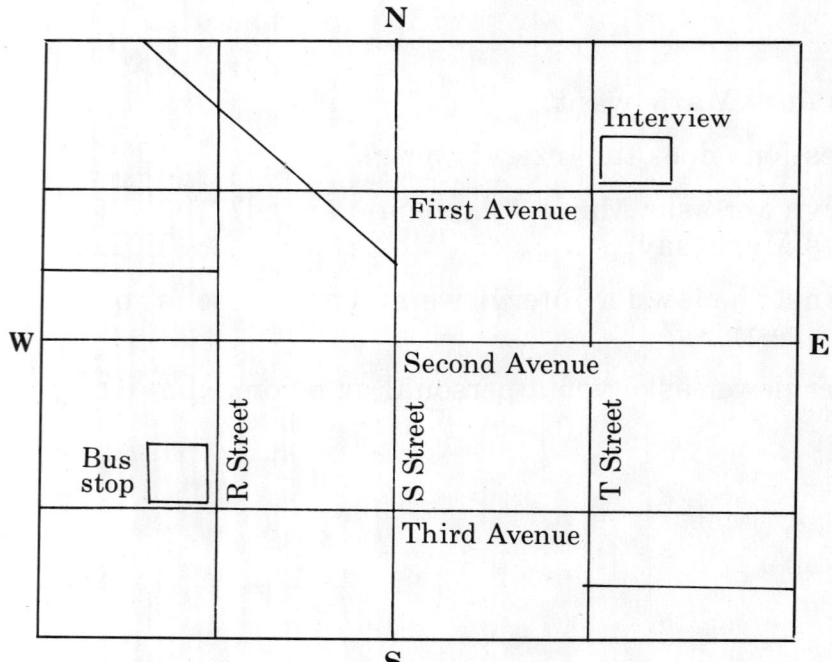

WORDS FOR WORK

north	left	go
south	right	turn
east	blocks	
west	corner	

Practice

Look at the map and tell how to get from the first place to the second place.

Example:

Bus stop—copy shop

Go one block north on R Street. Turn right on Second Avenue and go one block.

1. post office—school
2. school—restaurant
3. hospital—post office
4. bank—hospital
5. Bus stop—school

JOB APPLICATIONS

When you apply for a job, you must fill out a job application. Read this portion of a sample job application.

Job Application

Date: __4/15/91__

Social Security Number: __123-45-6789__

Name: __Diaz__, __Graciela__ _____
     (Last)   (First)   (Middle)

Address: __201__ __R Street__
    (Number)   (Street)

__Chicago__ __IL__ __60640__
(City)   (State)   (Zip Code)

Phone: __(312)__ __555-2456__
   (Area Code)

Signature: __Graciela Diaz__

Now fill one out for yourself.

Job Application

Date: _____

Social Security Number: _____

Name: _____
   (Last)   (First)   (Middle)

Address: _____
   (Number)   (Street)

_____
(City)   (State)   (Zip Code)

Phone: _____
   (Area Code)

Signature: _____

STRUCTURE WORK

Part 1

Write *What, When, Where, Who,* or *How* in each of the blanks to complete the questions. Some sentences have more than one word that fits. Follow the example.

1. <u>Where</u> do you work?
2. _____ long have you been at your job?
3. _____ old are you?
4. _____ can you start work?
5. _____ did you do at your last job?
6. _____ is your religion?
7. _____ is your height?
8. _____ country are you from?
9. _____ is your husband's job?
10. _____ much experience do you have?

Part 2

Remember that personal questions are not legal. Have a partner ask you the questions above. If the question is legal, answer it. If the question is not legal, say, "I'd rather not answer that." Your teacher will demonstrate.

PROBLEM SOLVING

Looking Good

At a job interview in the U.S., it's important to:

- ☑ dress properly
- ☑ look neat and clean
- ☑ make eye contact
- ☑ come on time
- ☑ show respect
- ☑ be polite
- ☑ act like you want the job
- ☑ show that you work well with others

1. In the U.S., what must you do to dress properly? look neat and clean? show respect?

2. Have you ever been to a job interview? What was it like?

3. Look at the pictures below. Both people are interviewing for the same job. Which person will get the job? Why?

Which One Would You Hire?

Read or listen to each interview. There are three applicants for a job as a cashier. What does each person do well? What does each person need to improve?

Mr. Connors: Have you ever worked as a cashier before?

Carlos: No, but I'm good with numbers and I like people.

Mr. Connors: Good.

Carlos: Are you looking for someone to work part-time?

Mr. Connors: Yes.

Carlos: I can work part-time. I can work in the afternoons and the evenings.

Mr. Connors: Good.

Mr. Connors: Why did you apply for this job as a cashier?

Duc: I need the money.

Mr. Connors: Would this be your second job?

Duc: Yes. In the mornings I'm a cashier in another restaurant, and I want to work here in the evenings.

Mr. Connors: I see. Do you like your other job?

Duc: No.

Mr. Connors: Have you worked as a cashier before, Choy?

Choy: I'm sorry. Could you repeat that?

Mr. Connors: Sure. Have you worked as a cashier before?

Choy: Yes. I worked as a cashier for a year and a half.

Mr. Connors: When can you start work?

Choy: On Monday.

Chapter 5
Pay and Benefits

WHAT ARE THE BENEFITS?

Look and Listen

Daniel: Can you tell me about the benefits?

Mr. Sanchez: You'll get health insurance, eight paid holidays, and one week paid vacation after a year of employment.

Daniel: Will I get life insurance?

Mr. Sanchez: No. You must buy your own life insurance.

Daniel: What about sick days?

Mr. Sanchez: You get six sick days a year.

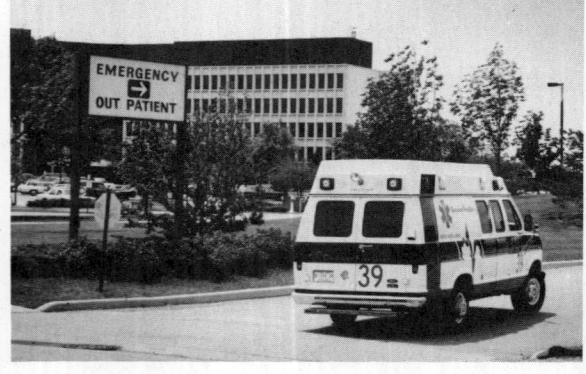

Check Your Understanding

Match each term to its definition.

___ 1. health insurance

___ 2. life insurance

___ 3. dental insurance

___ 4. sick days

___ 5. paid holidays

___ 6. paid vacation

a. time off when you are sick

b. pays doctor's bills

c. pays you on holidays when you don't work

d. pays your family if you die

e. pays for time off from work

f. pays dentist's bills

Practice

Interview three classmates. Ask them what benefits they want most.

Name	Most important benefits

WHEN DO I GET PAID?

Look and Listen

Daniel: When do I get paid?

Mr. Sanchez: You'll be paid on the first and the fifteenth of every month.

Daniel: Is the pay by the week or by the hour?

Mr. Sanchez: You'll be paid $6.50 an hour.

Daniel: What about overtime pay?

Mr. Sanchez: You'll get time and a half for overtime.

Check Your Understanding

Answer the questions.

1. When will Daniel get paid?
2. Will Daniel be paid by the hour or by the week?
3. How much will Daniel make per hour?
4. Will he get overtime pay? How much?

Forms of Pay

1. Some jobs pay by the hour. That's **hourly pay**. If you work more hours, you make more money. But the number of hours is not guaranteed. On other jobs, you get a **salary**, or fixed amount of money each year.

    Which do you prefer, and why? Check (✓) one. Discuss your choice with three other students.
    ____ salary
    ____ hourly pay

2. On some jobs, you get extra money for working overtime. This benefit is called **paid overtime**. On other jobs, you get compensation time, or **comp time**. You don't get more money, but you can take time off during the regular working day.

    Which do you prefer, and why? Check (✓) one. Discuss your choice with three other students.
    ____ paid overtime
    ____ comp time

VOCABULARY

Match the words with the pictures. Write the correct words under each picture. Follow the example.

| maternity leave | dental insurance | paid holidays |
| health insurance | paid vacation | sick days |

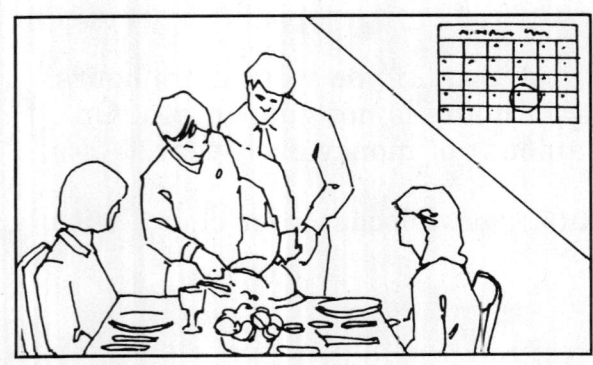

1. _paid holidays_

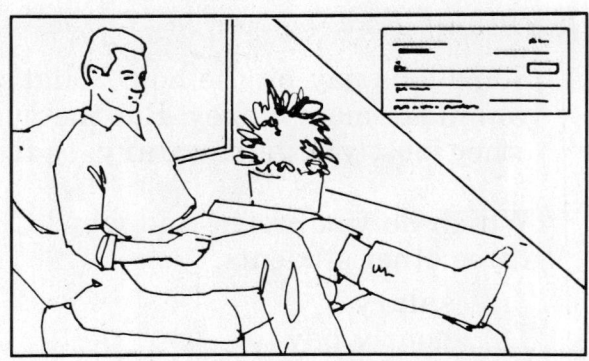

4. _____

2. _____

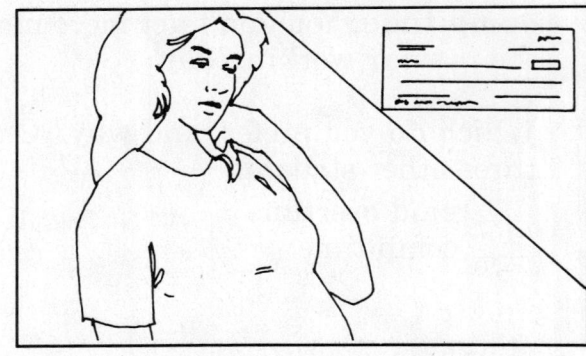

5. _____

3. _____

6. _____

TALKING TOGETHER

Do you think benefits are important?

If you support children or other relatives, you may want life insurance.

If you are married, you may not need health insurance. Your husband's or wife's health insurance may cover you.

Practice

What benefits do these people need? Read each story and decide. Work in groups.

Benefits They Need

1. My name is Carol Hong.
   I'm 23 years old.
   I'm single.
   I live with my parents.

2. My name is Marcelo Cruz.
   I'm 31 years old.
   I'm married, but I don't have children.
   I want to make a lot of money.

3. My name is Joe Berenz.
   I'm 44 years old.
   I'm married.
   I have two children.
   My son is 10, and my daughter is 15.
   My wife is working now.
   She has good health insurance at her job.

WORDS FOR WORK

hourly pay	hours	gross pay	net pay
salary	rate	pay period	income tax
overtime	earnings	pay date	federal
comp time	deduction	pay stub	state

Practice

Read the pay stub and answer the questions.

P A Y S T A T E M E N T			Social Security No. 204-15-0132	Name Gomez, Daniel					Pay Period ENDING 4/05/91		Pay Date 4/10/91
	Hours/Units	Rate	Earnings		Type	Deduction		Type	Deduction		Type
	80 00	6 50	520 00		REG	15 75		HEALTH	463 48		CHECK
	7 00	9 75	68 25		OVERTIME						
	This Pay	Gross Pay 588.25	Federal Income Tax 53.31		Social Security Tax 40.05	State Income Tax 15.66		Local Income Tax	SUI/SDI		Net Pay 479.23
	YTD										

1. What is the person's name?
2. What is the pay date of the check?
3. What deductions were taken from the check?
4. What is the gross pay? What is the net pay?
5. How much is deducted for federal taxes? for state taxes?
6. How many hours did the person work?

PARTNER WORK

Person 1

	Social Security No.	Name		Pay Period	Pay Date
		Cruz, Marcelo		ENDING	5/14/91
Hours/Units	Rate	Earnings	Type	Deduction	Type	Deduction	Type
80 00	5 50		REG		HEALTH		CHECK
				15 00	DENTAL		
					LIFE		
This Pay	Gross Pay	Federal Income Tax	Social Security Tax	State Income Tax	Local Income Tax	SUI/SDI	Net Pay
			14.05	12.60			
YTD							

Part 1

Ask your partner questions to fill out the pay stub. Your partner's questions are on page 58.

1. What is the social security number?
2. What is the pay period end date?
3. How much was deducted for health insurance?
4. How much was deducted for life insurance?
5. How much was the gross pay?
6. How much was the federal income tax?
7. How much were the regular earnings?

Part 2

Now calculate the pay.

1. How much is the net pay (gross pay minus taxes and social security)?
2. How much is the check (net pay minus deductions for health, life, and dental insurance)?

fifty-seven

Person 2

P A Y		Social Security No 315-40-0506	Name			Pay Period ENDING 5/11/91	Pay Date
S T A T E M E N T	Hours/Units	Rate	Earnings	Type	Deduction	Type	Deduction	Type
			440|00	REG	12|74 6|00	HEALTH DENTAL LIFE		CHECK
	This Pay	Gross Pay 440.00	Federal Income Tax 39.50	Social Security Tax	State Income Tax	Local Income Tax	SUI/SDI	Net Pay
	YTD							

Part 1

Ask your partner questions to fill out the pay stub. Your partner's questions are on page 57.

1. What is the person's name?
2. What is the pay date?
3. How many hours did the person work?
4. What is the rate of pay?
5. How much is the social security tax?
6. How much is the state income tax?
7. How much was deducted for dental insurance?

Part 2

Now calculate the pay.

1. How much is the net pay (gross pay minus taxes and social security)?
2. How much is the check (net pay minus deductions for health, life, and dental insurance)?

STRUCTURE WORK

Which is correct?
1. How **many** tools do you have?
2. How **much** tools do you have?

The first sentence is correct. The word *many* is used with things that can be counted: 1 tool, 2 tools, 3 tools.

Which of these is correct?
1. How **many** money do you have?
2. How **much** money do you have?

Sentence 2 is correct. You can't say, "1 money, 2 money, 3 money." The word *much* is used with words that are not plural and cannot be counted.

> how many + _____s (plural)
> how much + no plural

Practice

Choose *much* or *many*.

1. How **much** paid vacation time do I have?
2. How _____ holidays do I have?
3. How _____ life insurance do I have?
4. How _____ days a year do I have?
5. How _____ sick leave do I have?
6. How _____ days of paid vacation do I have?
7. How _____ years have you worked there?
8. How _____ weeks were you off?

PROBLEM SOLVING

Employment Record

Name: **Lopez, Enrique**

Company Name	Job	Duties	Dates of Employment
Fix-All Auto Repair	mechanic	give estimates, repair cars, handle customers	5/86–present
Speedy Transport Taxi Co.	taxi driver	drove a taxi, made change, reported to dispatcher	1/84–4/86
Sunshine Restaurant	busboy	cleared tables, washed dishes	3/81–12/83

Answer the questions.

1. What three jobs are on the employment record?
2. Where is Enrique Lopez working now?
3. How long was he a taxi driver?
4. Was he ever unemployed for more than a month?
5. What are Enrique's duties as a mechanic?
6. Where did Enrique work in 1982?
7. What job did he hold the longest?
8. In what order are the jobs listed?
9. Do you think Enrique would be a good bus driver? Why or why not?

Write About Your Jobs

1. The time line below shows all of the jobs Enrique Lopez has held. Read the time line. Then write a time line of all your jobs.

```
came
to U.S.A    busboy           taxi driver—        Mechanic—
                             Speedy              Fix-All
                             Transport           Auto
   |          |                 |                   |         |
  1980       1981              1984                1986    present
```

2. Fill in the employment record below with your job information.

Employment Record

Name: _____

Company Name	Job	Duties	Dates of Employment

What job did you like the most? Why?

Was it different from the job you have now?

sixty-one 61

Chapter 6
Talking with Coworkers

HOW'S IT GOING WITH THE NEW JOB?

Look and Listen

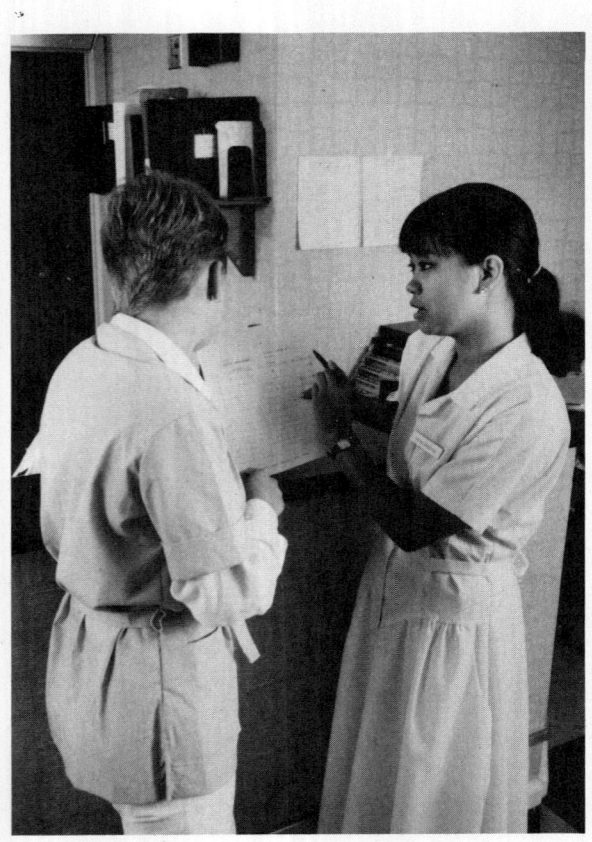

Mei: Hi, Zosia. How's it going with the new job?

Zosia: Not bad. There sure is a lot to learn.

Mei: Do you have any questions?

Zosia: Well, there is one thing.

Mei: What's that?

Zosia: Where do I write my sick day on my time sheet?

Mei: Let me show you. Right here.

Zosia: Oh, that's right. Thank you.

Mei: You're welcome. Don't worry. You'll do fine.

Zosia: I hope so. Thanks again.

Check Your Understanding

Circle Yes or No.

1. Zosia and Mei work in a hospital.   Yes   No
2. Zosia has worked at the hospital a long time.   Yes   No
3. Zosia is holding a job application.   Yes   No
4. Mei wants to help Zosia.   Yes   No
5. Zosia forgot where to write her vacation time.   Yes   No

Practice

1. Practice asking for help:
   Excuse me. Can you help me?
   Please help me with this.
   Could you help me with this, please?
   Could you give me a hand?
   I need your help for a minute, please.

2. Which questions would you ask a friend or coworker? Which would you ask your boss? Write the questions in the chart.

	Asking for help
Friend or coworker	
Boss	

3. Now practice two dialogues—one with a coworker and one with your boss. Use different questions to ask for help.

○ Excuse me. Can you help me?
● Sure.
○ Thank you.
● You're welcome.

WHAT ARE YOU DOING THIS WEEKEND?

Look and Listen

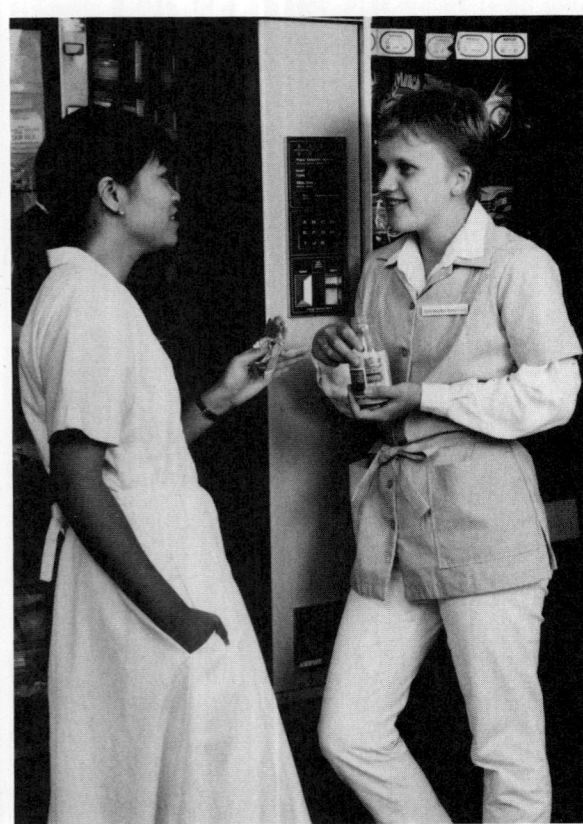

Zosia: What are you doing this weekend?

Mei: I'm going to a party with my husband.

Zosia: That sounds like fun.

Mei: What are you going to do, Zosia?

Zosia: I don't know. Maybe I'll go to the movies.

Mei: Look, it's 10:30. My break's over.

Zosia: See you later!

Mei: Bye.

Check Your Understanding

Circle Yes or No.

1. Mei and Zosia are on break.	Yes	No
2. They are talking about work.	Yes	No
3. Mei is going to go to a party.	Yes	No
4. Zosia is going to go on vacation.	Yes	No
5. Mei's break ends at 10:30.	Yes	No

Practice

You and a coworker are talking on a Friday afternoon. Complete the following conversation with the words on page 66 or your own words.

You:
What are you doing this weekend?

Coworker:
I'm _____. How about you?

You:
I think I'm _____.

Coworker:
That sounds like fun. Have a nice weekend!

You:
Thanks. You too.

VOCABULARY

Write the correct words under each picture.

1. _____

4. _____

2. _____

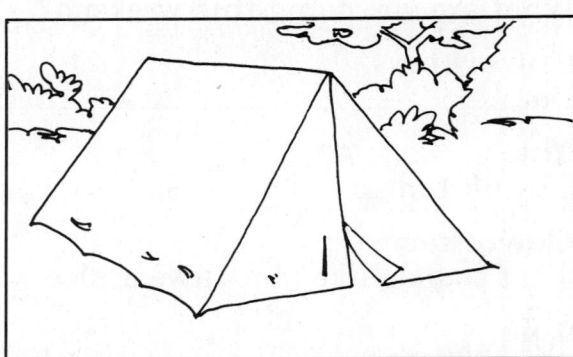

5. _____

3. _____

6. _____

- going shopping
- going camping
- going bicycling

- going to a party
- going to the movies
- going to visit the family

TALKING TOGETHER

Read the time sheet below. Then answer the questions.

	In	Out	In	Out	Hours Worked
\multicolumn{6}{	c	}{Time Sheet}
\multicolumn{6}{	l	}{Name: Zosia Mazwiek Pay Period Ending: 4/21/91}
Sat.	—	—	—	—	—
Sun.	3 p.m.	7 p.m.	8 p.m.	11 p.m.	7
Mon.	3 p.m.	7 p.m.	8 p.m.	11 p.m.	7
Tues.	—	—	—	—	P
Wed.	7 a.m.	11 a.m.	11:30 a.m.	3 p.m.	7½
Thurs.	7 a.m.	11 a.m.	11:30 a.m.	3 p.m.	7½
Fri.	7 a.m.	11 a.m.	11:30 a.m.	3 p.m.	7½

Total 36½

If not worked indicate: P—Personal/sick   V—Vacation   C—Comp day
H—Holiday

1. Whose name is on the time sheet?
2. When did she start work on Monday—at 3 P.M. or 7 P.M.?
3. When did she leave work on Monday?
4. On Thursday, how long was her break?
5. What day was she sick?
6. What was her day off?

WORDS FOR WORK

time sheet	start
vacation	leave
holiday	lunch
break	total

Write the correct abbreviations for the days of the week.

Sunday _____

Monday _____

Tuesday _____

Wednesday _____

Thursday _____

Friday _____

Saturday _____

About You

1. When do you start work? _____
2. When do you leave work? _____
3. When is your break? _____
4. What do you do on your break? _____
5. This year, when is your vacation? _____
6. What are you going to do on your vacation? _____

SPEAKING PRACTICE

Write out each of the conversations. Practice with a partner. Use your real names.

1. **A:** Hi, _____. How's _____ new job?
   B: Not bad. But there _____ a lot to learn.
   A: Do you have any _____?
   B: There is one thing.
   A: What's _____?
   B: Where _____?
   A: Let me _____ you.

2. **A:** What are you _____ this weekend?
   B: I think I'm going _____.
   A: That _____ like fun. Have a nice weekend!
   B: You, too.

3. **A:** Hi, _____. Can you help me with this?
   B: Not now. Sorry.
   A: OK. Thanks anyway.
   B: Maybe someone else can _____ you.
   A: I'll _____ Lisette.

SPEAKING PRACTICE

Make a conversation using the sentences and questions below. Then practice it with a partner.

Person A	Person B
I'm going camping with my family.	Pretty good. What are you up to this weekend?
Hi. How's it going?	That sounds great! How is your family?
They're doing fine. My son is playing baseball, and my daughter is learning to drive.	OK. See you later.
Well, I have to go now.	My son likes baseball, too.

A: _____

B: _____

A: _____

B: _____

A: _____

B: _____

A: _____

B: _____

STRUCTURE WORK

Part 1

Complete each question with one of the words below.

where what can how

1. <u>What</u> are you going to do this weekend?
2. _____ is Mei's occupation?
3. _____ you help me?
4. _____ about giving me a hand?
5. _____ you help me fill out my time sheet?
6. _____ you get someone else to help you?
7. _____ are you going on your vacation?
8. _____ is your family?
9. _____ time do you finish work?
10. _____ many hours a day do you work?

Part 2

Complete the questions with *going to do*. Then answer the questions with any words from the list below.

going to a party	going bicycling
going to the movies	going camping
going to visit the family	going shopping

Example: What's Miranda *going to do*?
She's *going camping*.

1. What's Noriko _____?
   She's _____.
2. What's Enrique _____?
   He's _____.
3. What are you _____?
   I'm _____.

PROBLEM SOLVING

What's the Story?

What are they saying?

1.

2.
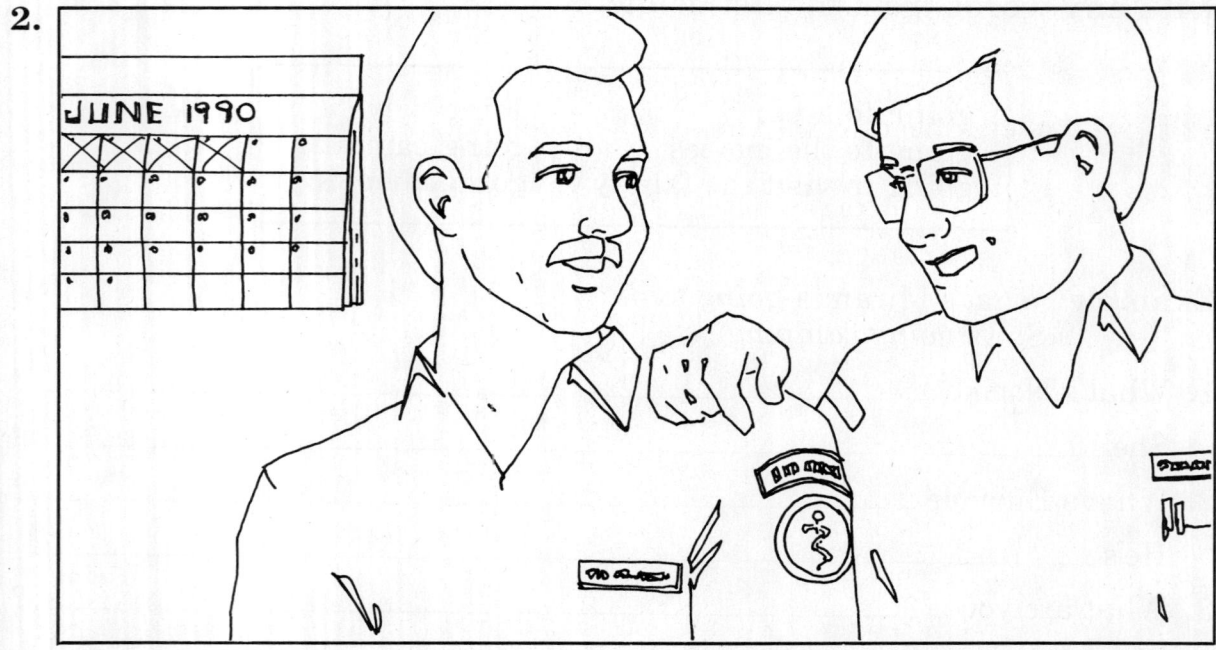

Is Something Wrong?

Mei and Zosia are talking in the cafeteria. Finish their conversation and then act it out.

Mei: Hi, Zosia. May I sit here?

Zosia: OK.

Mei: How's it going?

Zosia: I'm fine.

Mei: How's your husband doing in his new job?

Zosia: He's doing fine.

Mei: Is something wrong?

Zosia: No—I just don't want to talk right now.

Mei: _____

Zosia: _____

Answer the questions.
1. Where are Mei and Zosia?
2. What does Mei want to do?
3. Do you think Zosia is unfriendly? Why or why not?
4. How does Mei feel? How does Zosia feel?
5. Have you ever been in this situation? What happened?

Chapter 7
Asking Questions at Work

HOW MANY TOWELS DO I NEED?

Look and Listen

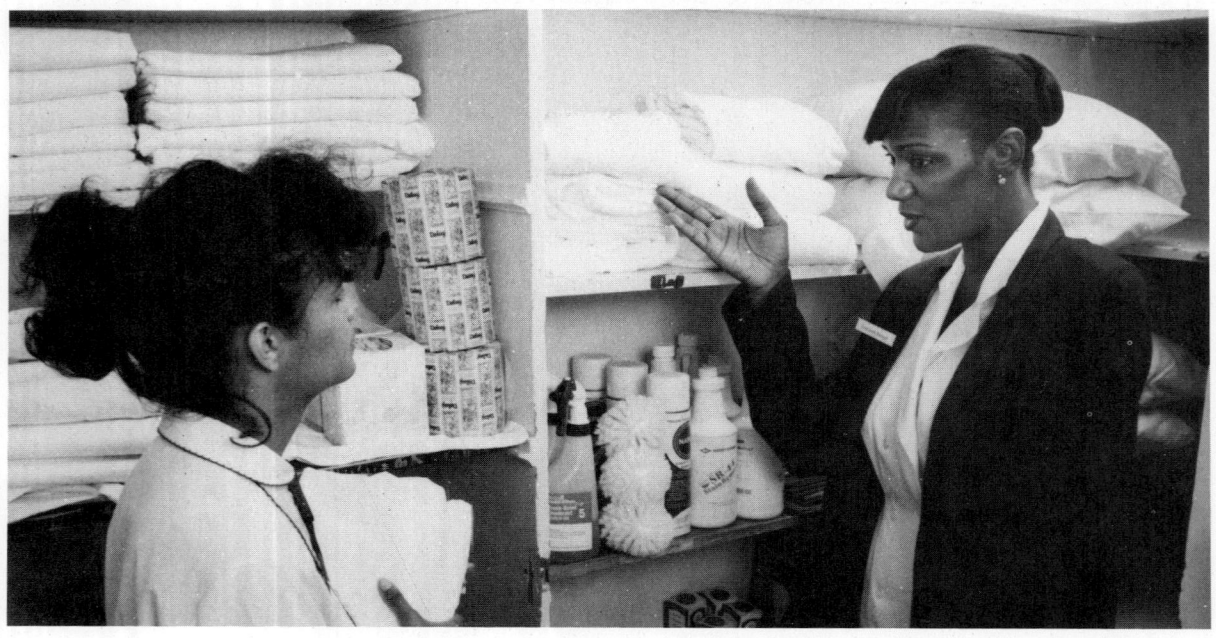

Ms. Smith: This is the storage room. Come here first every day and stock your cart.

Maria: What supplies will I need?

Ms. Smith: Well, this cart is almost full now. But it needs vacuum cleaner bags.

Maria: Where are the vacuum cleaner bags?

Ms. Smith: On the bottom shelf.

Maria: Where? I don't see them.

Ms. Smith: There, next to the light bulbs.

Check Your Understanding

Write Yes or No.

_____ 1. The storage room is for supplies.

_____ 2. Maria is a new employee.

_____ 3. Maria will put supplies on the cart every morning.

_____ 4. The cart needs vacuum cleaner bags.

_____ 5. The vacuum cleaner bags are on the top shelf.

Practice

Make a list of things you think Maria needs on her cart. Choose from the words below.

storage room	towels	shelf
soap	vacuum cleaner	light bulbs
sheets	trash	room
vacuum cleaner bags	cleanser	

She needs:

_____   _____

_____   _____

_____   _____

_____

I THINK YOU'LL DO WELL ON YOUR JOB

Look and Listen

Ms. Smith: Do you know how to make a hotel bed?

Maria: Yes, I think so. Can you please watch me?

Ms. Smith: Sure. Let's do it right now.

Maria: What else should I do in each room?

Ms. Smith: Vacuum the floors, make the beds, clean the sink, empty the trash, and leave six clean towels.

Maria: Do I change light bulbs?

Ms. Smith: Yes. They're in the storage room, too. I think you'll do well on your job, Maria.

Practice

Use each word in the box correctly in the sentences below. Then practice speaking with a partner.

> leave   change   vacuum   empty   make

Ms. Smith: Please clean all the rooms on the first and second floors.

Maria: OK.

Ms. Smith: Please _____ the floors, _____ the beds, _____ the trash, _____ clean towels, and _____ the burned-out light bulbs.

Maria: OK, Ms. Smith, I'll take care of it right away.

Check Your Understanding

Answer the questions. Use a complete short answer.

Example: Are the supplies in the storage room?
   Yes, they are.

1. Is Maria a new employee?
2. Is Ms. Smith a new employee?
3. Should Maria leave eight towels in each room?
4. Should Maria change light bulbs?
5. Where are the light bulbs?
6. Does Ms. Smith like Maria?

VOCABULARY

Match each picture with the correct words.

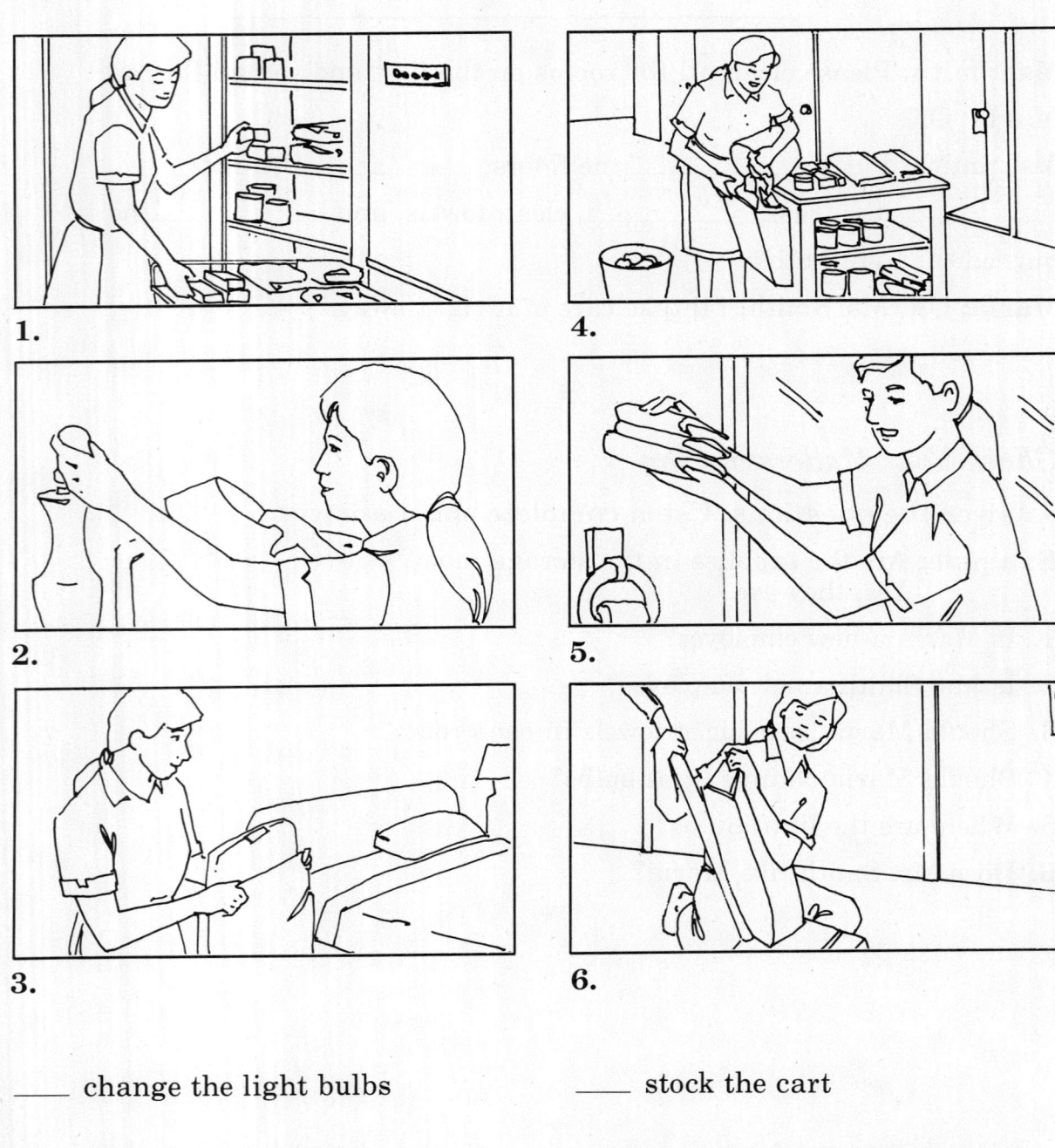

___ change the light bulbs

___ make the beds

___ empty the trash

___ stock the cart

___ change the vacuum cleaner bag

___ leave clean towels

TALKING TOGETHER

Circle the letter of the correct answer. Work in pairs.

1. Find the item you think Maria does *not* need on her cart.
   a. Vacuum cleaner bags
   b. Lamp
   c. Towels
   d. Soap

2. Find the question you think Maria should *not* ask her supervisor.
   a. Do I change the light bulbs?
   b. Where are the towels?
   c. If I finish my work early, can I go home?
   d. What else should I do?

3. Find the job you think Maria does *not* do.
   a. Wash the windows
   b. Clean the sink with cleanser
   c. Take out the dirty towels
   d. Put new soap next to the sink

4. What do you think Maria does *not* need to know?
   a. Where the storage room is
   b. How to change a vacuum cleaner bag
   c. How to fix a sink
   d. How to change sheets

WORDS FOR WORK

Part 1

Write each of the following words in the correct list.

supplies	bottom	next to
on	change	see
soap	sheets	cleanser
vacuum cleaner	leave	light bulbs
make	towels	watch
	stock	

Things in a storage room   **Action words**   **Location words**

_____   _____   _____
_____   _____   _____
_____   _____   _____
_____   _____   _____
_____   _____
_____   _____

Part 2

Fill in the blanks with words from the list below.

Every morning, Maria goes to the _____ 1 _____ and unlocks the door with her ___ 2 ___. She ___ 3 ___ her cart with sheets, ___ 4 ___, soap, and ___ 5 ___. Then she ___ 6 ___ the beds, ___ 7 ___ the trash, and ___ 8 ___ clean towels in all of the rooms on the ___ 9 ___ and ___ 10 ___ floors.

| makes | key | cleanser | empties | stocks |
| first | towels | leaves | second | storage room |

PARTNER WORK

Person 1

Part 1

Complete the inventory sheet below. Your partner has the missing information. Ask your partner:

How many <u>small towels</u>   are there?
　　　　sheets
　　　　light bulbs
　　　　cans of cleanser

Write the numbers on your chart.

Storage Room Inventory	
Large towels	54
Small towels	
Washcloths	24
Sheets	
Bars of soap	60
Light bulbs	
Vacuum cleaner bags	36
Cans of cleanser	

Part 2

Work with your partner to answer these questions.

1. Each room needs two sheets. There are enough sheets for how many rooms?

2. Each room needs four small towels. There are enough towels for how many rooms?

3. Is it more important for the storage room to get more sheets or more small towels?

PARTNER WORK

Person 2

Part 1

Complete the inventory sheet below. Your partner has the missing information. Ask your partner:

How many *large towels* are there?
          washcloths
          bars of soap
          vacuum cleaner bags

Write the numbers.

Storage Room Inventory	
Large towels	
Small towels	40
Washcloths	
Sheets	88
Bars of soap	
Light bulbs	24
Vacuum cleaner bags	
Cans of cleanser	25

Part 2

Work with your partner to answer these questions.

1. Each room needs two washcloths. There are enough washcloths for how many rooms?

2. Each room needs three bars of soap. There are enough bars of soap for how many rooms?

3. Can the housekeeper stock more rooms with washcloths or with soap?

STRUCTURE WORK

Write the correct form of the verb in each blank.

Example: Maria sometimes *changes* light bulbs.

1. She _____ (*leave*) clean towels every day.
2. Juan _____ (*take out*) the dirty towels once a day.
3. Yesterday, Ms. Smith _____ (*watch*) Maria change a vacuum cleaner bag.
4. Ming can _____ (*fix*) a faucet.
5. The housekeepers _____ (*stock*) their carts every morning.
6. Maria _____ (*make*) the beds before she takes out the trash.
7. She can _____ (*change*) a vacuum cleaner bag.
8. First _____ (*vacuum*) the floor, then clean the sink.
9. Do you know how to _____ (*wash*) windows?
10. When you finish cleaning the sink, please _____ (*empty*) the trash.

PROBLEM SOLVING

Boss or Worker?

Read each question. If the question is one you ask a boss, write *B*. If you should ask another worker, write *W*. For some questions, you may mark both.

_____ 1. I'm having trouble finishing my work. What should I do?

_____ 2. Excuse me. Where's the cleanser?

_____ 3. Maria sometimes wants me to do her work. What should I do?

_____ 4. Does my health insurance cover my family, too?

_____ 5. Where should I put my time sheet?

_____ 6. Can I take my vacation from September 4 to September 15?

_____ 7. How many bars of soap go in each room?

_____ 8. Can I borrow a light bulb from your cart?

_____ 9. I have a dentist appointment tomorrow morning. Can I come to work at 11 A.M. and work late?

_____ 10. I can't make my key work in this door. Can you help me?

- At your job, who do you ask for help? Why?
- What questions do you ask at a new job?

Learning the Rules

Read the *Instructions to Employees* below. Then answer the questions.

Instructions to Employees

1. Report to work 15 minutes before your shift begins.

2. The time clock is next to the storage room. Punch the time clock when you arrive and when you leave work. Put your time sheet in the slot. Sign your time sheet every week.

3. Stock your cart with the following:

16 large towels	24 bars of soap
16 small towels	4 light bulbs
16 washcloths	2 vacuum cleaner bags
20 sheets	1 can of cleanser

   Report any missing supplies to your supervisor.

4. Before entering rooms, knock on doors and say, "Housekeeping."

5. Report any damaged or missing items in rooms to your supervisor.

---

1. Where is the time clock?
2. Maria's shift begins at 8:00 A.M. She punches in at 7:50. Is she late?
3. Maria has eight bars of soap on her cart. There are eight more in the storage room. What should she do?
4. Maria needs to clean Room 204. She thinks no one is in there. What should she do?
5. She sees a stain on the carpet in Room 129. What should she do?

- What are some rules at your job?
- How do you learn rules at a new job?

Chapter 8
Reporting Absence

I THINK I HAVE THE FLU

Look and Listen

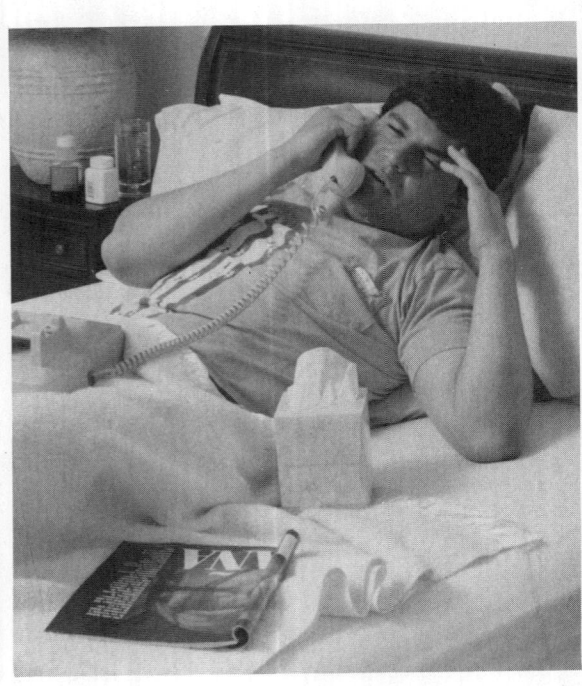 

Mr. Carter: Hello. Central Plating. This is Mr. Carter speaking.

Juan: This is Juan Torres. I'm sorry. I can't come to work today.

Mr. Carter: Oh? What's the matter?

Juan: I have a fever and a bad headache. I think I have the flu.

Mr. Carter: That's too bad. Get some rest. I hope you feel better.

Juan: Thank you.

Check Your Understanding

Circle the correct answer.

1. Who is talking to Juan on the phone?

    a coworker   his boss

2. Where does Juan work?

    in a hospital   at Central Plating

3. What's the matter with Juan? (You may choose more than one word.)

    cough   backache   earache   headache   stomachache   fever

4. What does Juan's boss tell him to do?

    get some rest   go to a doctor

5. Is Juan going to work today?

    yes   no

Practice

Write the words below in the blanks.

> work   call
> speak sick

Juan: Hello. May I _____ to Mr. Carter?

Mr. Carter: This is Mr. Carter.

Juan: This is Juan Torres. I'm _____. I can't come to _____ today.

Mr. Carter: Thanks for calling. Please _____ me tomorrow if you're still sick.

Juan: OK. I will.

I'M GOING TO BE LATE

Look and Listen

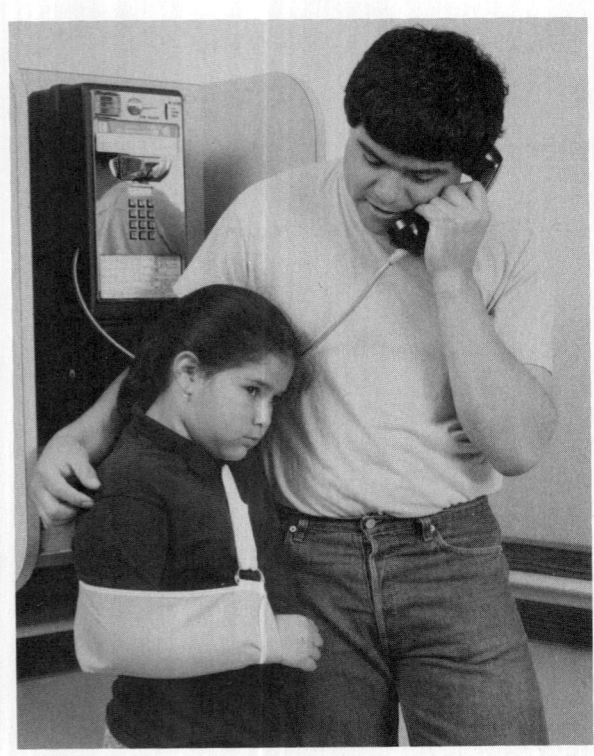

Bob: Central Plating. This is Bob speaking.

Juan: This is Juan Torres. May I speak to Mr. Carter?

Bob: I'm sorry, Juan. He isn't here right now.

Juan: Could I leave a message, please? Tell him I'm going to be late to work today because my daughter broke her arm.

Bob: I'm sorry to hear that. Could you spell your last name, please?

Juan: T-o-r-r-e-s.

Bob: OK. I've got it. I'll give him the message.

Practice

Match the pictures with the correct words.

a.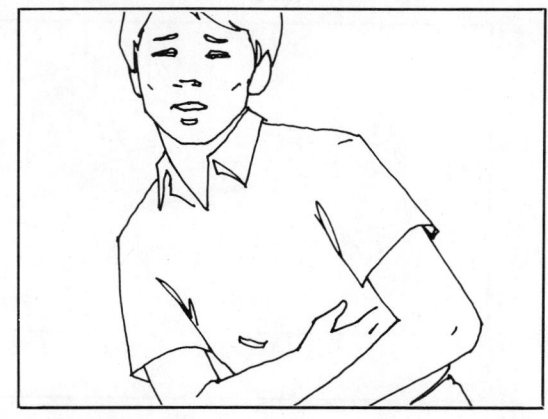

d.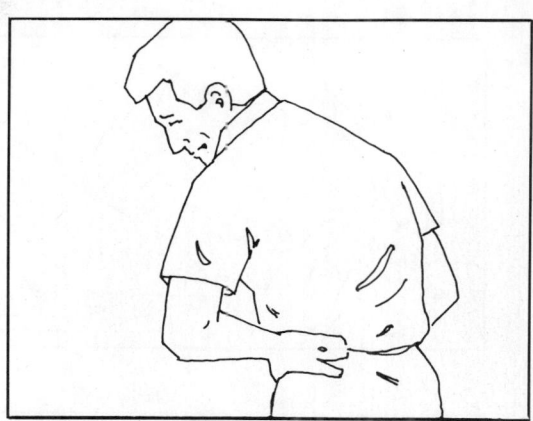

b.

e.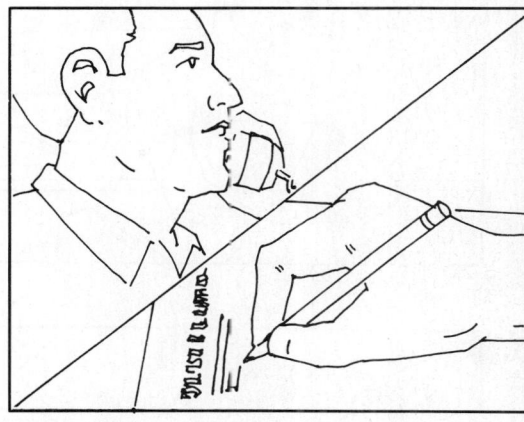

c.

f.

____ 1. She has a fever.

____ 2. He has a backache.

____ 3. He has a stomachache.

____ 4. He has an earache.

____ 5. He's leaving a message.

____ 6. She's calling in sick.

VOCABULARY

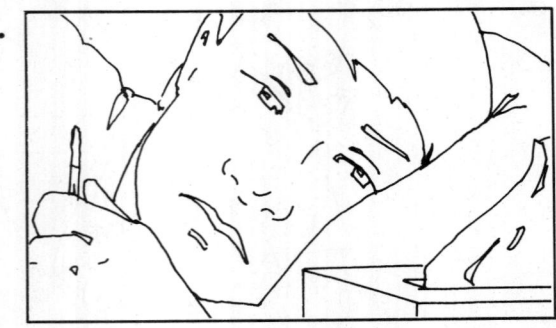

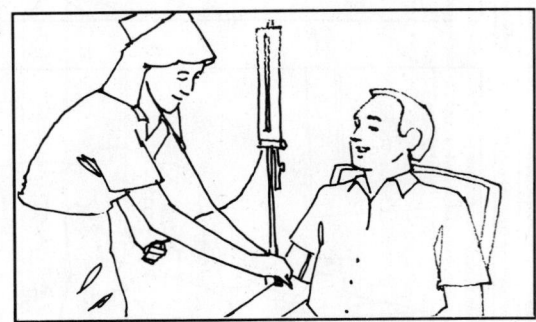

Match each phrase to the correct picture.

____ My car broke down.

____ I have to go to a funeral.

____ I have to go to court.

____ I have to go to the airport.

____ I have a doctor's appointment.

____ I'm sick.

TALKING TOGETHER

Make a conversation reporting a need to leave work early. Use the questions and sentences below or make up your own. Then practice with a partner.

Juan
No, I couldn't. But I can come in early tomorrow morning.

I have a doctor's appointment tomorrow at 3 P.M. I have to leave early.

Thank you, Mr. Carter.

Mr. Carter
Yes, Juan. What is it?

OK. That would be fine.

Oh? You couldn't get an appointment on your day off?

Juan: *Mr. Carter, may I speak to you for a moment, please?*

Mr. Carter: _____
Juan: _____

Mr. Carter: _____
Juan: _____

Mr. Carter: _____
Juan: _____

WORDS FOR WORK

Part 1

Which word does *not* belong? Cross out the word.

1. headache   earache   backache   message
2. speak   stomachache   rest   come
3. spell   leave   call   earache
4. stomachache   flu   headache   backache
5. come   break   coworker   get

Part 2

Write each word below in the correct list.

coworker	earache	come	flu
speak	boss	get	stomachache
spell	headache	break	leave

Action Words   **Illnesses**   **People**

SPEAKING PRACTICE

Complete the conversations. Then practice in pairs. Use your real names. Give a variety of reasons for being absent or late.

1. **Worker:** This is _____ _____. I'm sorry. I can't come to work today.

   Boss: Oh? What's _____ _____?

   Worker: I have _____.

   Boss: That's _____. I hope you _____ _____.

   Worker: Thanks.

2. **Worker:** This is _____ _____. I'm going to be late to work today.

   Boss: Oh? What's _____ _____?

   Worker: I have _____.

   Boss: That's OK. Thanks for calling.

3. **Worker:** This is _____ _____. May I speak to _____?

   Coworker: I'm _____. He or She isn't _____ right now.

   Worker: Could I leave a _____, please? Tell him or her I _____ come to work today because _____.

   Coworker: Could you spell your last _____, please?

   Worker: _____.

   Coworker: OK. I've _____ it. I'll give him or her the message.

SPEAKING PRACTICE

Part 1

Read or listen to each reason. Write *A* if it is a reason for absence from work. Write *L* if it is a reason for being late. Explain your answers.

____ 1. My car won't start.

____ 2. I have the flu.

____ 3. I have to take my son to the dentist.

____ 4. My daughter cut her head. I have to take her to the doctor.

____ 5. My mother passed away.

____ 6. A burglar broke into my house.

____ 7. My sink is leaking. A plumber is coming.

____ 8. I have to go to court.

Part 2

Complete the statement below with a reason for being late or absent. Then give a time or date you'll be in to work. Practice with a partner.

Example: I'll be late to work today because <u>my car won't start</u>. I'll be in <u>at 11:00</u>.
OR
I can't come to work today because <u>my grandmother passed away</u>. I'll be in <u>on Thursday</u>.

Worker: I'll be late.

I can't come to work today because _____

_____.

I'll be in _____.

94   ninety-four

STRUCTURE WORK

Part 1

Choose the correct word to complete each sentence.

> has   is   have   am

Example: He __has__ a headache.

1. I _____ a temperature and a bad headache.
2. This _____ Juan Torres.
3. He _____ to go to the dentist.
4. I _____ in bed resting.
5. He _____ a backache.
6. She _____ calling in sick.
7. I think I _____ the flu.
8. He _____ leaving a message.
9. She _____ taking her son to the doctor.
10. She _____ an earache.

Part 2

Work with a partner. Ask your partner to leave a message for your boss saying that you won't be in to work. Give the reason. Say when you'll come back to work.

Message
To: _____
From: _____
Date: _____ Time: _____ A.M. / P.M.
_____
_____
_____

PROBLEM SOLVING

Ahead or Same Day?

Some reasons for being late or absent can be reported ahead of time. Some must be reported the same day. Check *ahead* or *same day* next to each reason below.

	Ahead	Same day
1. I have a dentist's appointment at 2 P.M. on Thursday.		
2. My mother is in the hospital. I need to leave early to see her.		
3. My car broke down.		
4. My daughter has the measles.		
5. My alarm didn't go off.		
6. I have to take my daughter to the eye doctor on Monday.		
7. I have a fever and a sore throat.		
8. I have to leave early to pick up my car at the shop.		
9. My brother is arriving from Mexico.		
10. I'm moving to a new apartment.		

Should You Go to Work?

Part 1

Should you go to work? Check the box. Explain your reason.

	Go to work	Stay home
1. Your son has a bad cold and needs to stay home from school.		
2. Your sister had a baby last week. She wants you to help at home.		
3. You don't feel sick, but you are very tired.		
4. Your father is very sick in the hospital, and you know he wants to see you.		
5. You have a doctor's appointment for 4 P.M. Your shift begins at 3 P.M.		
6. Your uncle is visiting you from your country.		
7. You have a bad cold. You call your boss to say that you are staying home. Your boss says she really needs you at work.		

Part 2

You call your boss to say you can't come to work because _____. Your boss doesn't think this is a good reason.

What would you say to your boss?

Discuss these questions.
- Why is it a good idea to report an absence as soon as you can?
- What happens if you don't report an absence?
- What happens if you are sick or late many times?
- What happens if you come to work when you are sick?

Chapter 9
Following Instructions

I'LL START ON IT RIGHT AWAY

Look and Listen

Mario: Han, I want you to unload all the flowers from the truck. Then plant them six inches apart over there.

Han: You mean over there next to the house?

Mario: No, there along the lawn.

Han: OK. About six inches apart?

Mario: That's right. Then make sure they get plenty of water.

Han: I'll start on it right away.

Check Your Understanding
Write Yes or No.

____ 1. The supervisor is a woman.

____ 2. The flowers are in the truck.

____ 3. Han is going to plant the flowers three inches apart.

____ 4. First he must unload the truck.

____ 5. The flowers go next to the house.

____ 6. Han is going to water the flowers.

____ 7. Han understands the instructions at first.

Practice
Write the words below in the blanks.

| plant | unload | give |

Mario: Han, please plant those flowers.

Han: No problem.

Mario: First, _____ the truck.

   Next, _____ the flowers six inches apart along the lawn.

   Then, _____ them plenty of water.

Han: OK.

WHAT'S NEXT?

Look and Listen

Han: I'm finished. I planted all the flowers. What's next?

Mario: You need to mow the lawn and trim the hedges.

Han: OK. I should cut the grass and trim the hedges.

Mario: That's right.

Han: I'll sweep the pavement too.

- How does Han show that he understands?
- Han offers to sweep the pavement even though Mario doesn't tell him to do it. Is this a good idea? Why or why not?

Practice

Number the pictures to match the order of the actions.

1. Mow the lawn, sweep the pavement, and turn on the sprinkler.

2. Unload the flowers, dig the holes, and plant the flowers.

3. Rake the leaves, trim the hedges, and weed the garden.

VOCABULARY

Circle the correct word. Then write it in the blank.

1. weed
   trim
   plant   _____

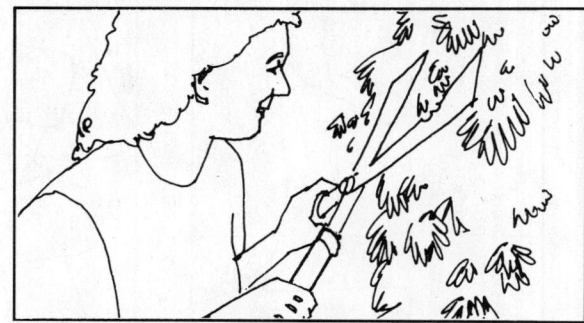

4. leaves
   flowers
   hedges   _____

2. unload
   rake
   mow   _____

5. lawn mower
   pavement
   sprinkler   _____

3. pavement
   sprinkler
   leaves   _____

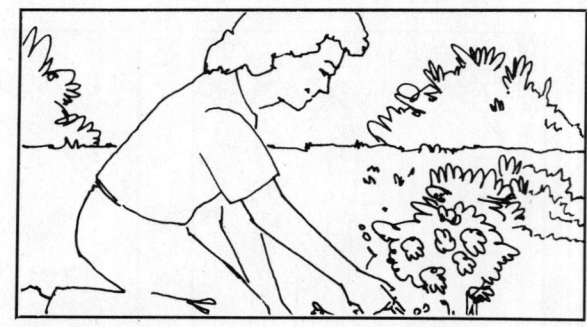

6. weed
   trim
   sweep   _____

TALKING TOGETHER

Part 1

Work in pairs. One student reads tasks from the checklist and the other acts them out. As each task is performed, the reader checks it off.

Task	Done?
Rake leaves	
Trim hedges	
Unload flowers	
Dig holes	
Plant flowers	
Mow lawn	
Sweep pavement	

Part 2

Now write tasks you do at work or at home on the checklist below. Have your partner read each task. Then act out the task and have your partner check it off the list.

Task	Done?

WORDS FOR WORK

Choose a word or pair of words from each list to form a command. Write as many commands as you can. Begin each command with a capital letter. Follow the example.

List 1	List 2
weed	the hedges
plant	the garden
sweep	the grass
mow	the flowers
turn on	the leaves
rake	the ground
dig	the pavement
water	the sprinkler
trim	the holes
turn off	the lawn

1. Weed the garden.
2.
3.
4.
5.
6.
7.
8.
9.
10.

SPEAKING PRACTICE

Practice the following conversations with a partner. In the second conversation use the tasks from the box in the blanks.

Conversation 1

A: Please sweep the pavement and put away the tools. Wait. There's something else. Before you sweep the pavement, please trim the hedges.

B: Excuse me. Could you repeat that?

A: Sorry. Please trim the hedges. Then sweep the pavement and put away the tools.

B: I trim the hedges, sweep the pavement, and then put away the tools.

A: Yes. Thank you.

Conversation 2

turn on the sprinkler	water the flowers
weed the garden	rake the leaves
trim the hedges	mow the lawn
dig the holes	plant the shrubs

A: Please _____ and _____.
   Wait. There's something else. Before you _____, please _____.

B: Excuse me. Could you repeat that?

A: Sorry. Please _____.
   Then _____ and _____.

B: I _____, _____, and then _____.

A: Yes. Thank you.

- How does the worker find out which task to do first?

NEW EXPRESSIONS

Your boss gives instructions to you in a certain way. When you give instructions to coworkers, you need to work together and not give orders. Look at the examples below.

The boss says:

        Please
    I want you to
  Make sure you   turn on the sprinkler.
  Don't forget to

Coworkers say:

          Let's
     Why don't we
The boss wants us to   turn on the sprinkler.
        Can you
      We need to
       Could you
         Please

Practice

Give instructions using the following descriptions.

Example: You are the boss. You want your helper to water the flowers.
          You say: *Please water the flowers.*

1. You are a worker. You want a coworker to pass you the rake.
   You say:

2. You are a worker. You want a coworker to help you carry the flowers.
   You say:

3. You are a worker. You want to tell a coworker to help you unload tools from the truck.
   You say:

4. You are the boss. You want to tell a worker not to use the lawn mower.
   You say:

5. You are the boss. You want to tell a worker to wear gloves while working.
   You say:

SPEAKING PRACTICE

Imagine you are the worker in the picture. A coworker is asking you questions. Answer the questions using *over here* or *over there*. Point to each object.

1. Where's the rake?
2. Where's the lawn mower?
3. Where's the wheelbarrow?
4. Where's the hose?
5. Where's the truck?

6. Where's the shovel?
7. Where are the hedge clippers?
8. Where are the gloves?
9. Where are the flowers?
10. Where's the broom?

PROBLEM SOLVING

A Change of Plans

Read each dialogue and then talk about what each worker said.

1. **Mario:** What are you doing, Han?

   Han: I'm watering the flowers.

   Mario: No. I told you to *weed* the flowers.

   Han: Sorry. I thought you said to water them.

2. **Han:** Hey, Ramon! You have to wear safety glasses when you use the blower to sweep the pavement.

   Ramon: But there aren't any in the truck.

   Han: You can use mine. I don't need them right now.

   Ramon: Thanks.

3. **Ramon:** What are you doing? Didn't the boss tell you to plant the flowers near the house?

   Han: I thought he said to plant them along the lawn.

   Ramon: He said to plant them near the house.

   Han: I'm going to ask him again.

- Have you ever misunderstood instructions? What happened?
- Do your coworkers ever tell you that you're not doing your job properly? What happens?

It's Not Safe!

Finish the conversations. Then act them out.

1. Han and Mario are working together.

    Mario: Please finish sweeping the pavement.

    Han: I'm sorry, but the dust is making my eyes hurt a lot.

    Mario: We have to finish by 5:00.

    Han: _____

2. Han and Paola, a coworker, are driving on the freeway in a truck. There are garden tools in the back of the truck.

    Paola: Do you hear that noise?

    Han: What noise?

    Paola: It's coming from the back of the truck.

    Han: Oh, yeah, I hear it. Well, we can't stop now. We'll be late.

    Paola: _____

3. Mario is talking to Han.

    Mario: Please mow the lawn, and use the new lawn mower.

    Han: Excuse me, but I don't know how to use it.

    Mario: I'm sure you can figure it out.

    Han: _____

- What do you do when your supervisor tells you to do something unsafe?
- What do you do when you see a coworker doing something unsafe?

Chapter 10
Asking for Help

THIS HAMBURGER ISN'T COOKED ENOUGH

Look and Listen

Rosa: Excuse me. The customer says this hamburger isn't cooked enough.

Tomás: Oh?

Rosa: She says she wants it well done. This is medium. Can you cook it a little longer, please?

Tomás: OK. I'll have it ready in a few minutes.

Rosa: Thanks. I really appreciate it.

Tomás: No problem.

Check Your Understanding

Circle Yes or No.

1. Tomás is a dishwasher.	Yes	No
2. Rosa is a waitress.	Yes	No
3. The customer says the hamburger is cooked too much.	Yes	No
4. The customer wants another hamburger.	Yes	No
5. Tomás is going to cook the hamburger a little longer.	Yes	No
6. Tomás and Rosa work well together.	Yes	No

Practice

Interview a partner. Share your answers with the class.

1. What is your job? _____
2. Do you have customers? _____
3. What problems do you have on your job? _____
4. Who can help you? How do you ask for help? _____
5. Do you work well with your coworkers? _____

THANKS FOR ALL YOUR HELP

Look and Listen

Rosa: Thank you for serving the water and the coffee so quickly, Mohammad.

Mohammad: You're welcome.

Rosa: Could you clear table five right now?

Mohammad: Sure.

Rosa: And table four needs more bread.

Mohammad: OK, Rosa.

Rosa: Thanks for all your help, Mohammad.

Practice

Read each situation. Decide how to ask politely for what you need. You may use these words or think of others.

> Excuse me.
> Can you please . . . ?
> Could you . . . ?
> Do you think you could . . . ?
> I think . . . .

Example: You are a waitress. You want the cook to cook a hamburger longer.
You say: *Can you please cook this hamburger longer?*

Example: You are a waiter. Your customer wanted whole wheat toast, not white. You want the cook to fix the order.
You say: *Excuse me. I think the customer wanted whole wheat toast, not white.*

1. You are a waiter or waitress. You want the busboy to fill the water glasses at table one.
   You say: _____

2. You are a cook. You want the waitress to explain an order you don't understand.
   You say: _____

3. You are a busboy. You want to ask the people at table two if they are finished.
   You say: _____

4. You are a dishwasher. You want to tell the supervisor there's a problem with the dishwashing machine.
   You say: _____

5. You are a customer. You want to tell your waiter that the total on your bill is incorrect.
   You say: _____

6. You are a waitress. Your customer says the total on her bill is incorrect. You check it. It is correct. You want the head waitress to tell her.
   You say: _____

VOCABULARY

Match each picture with the correct duty or duties. A picture can match more than one duty.

1. waitress

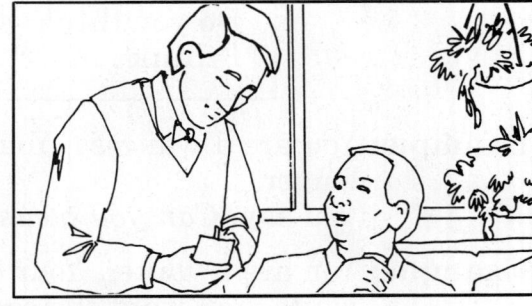

4. waiter

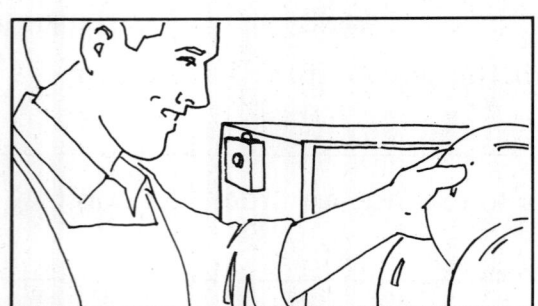

2. dishwasher

5. cook

3. busboy

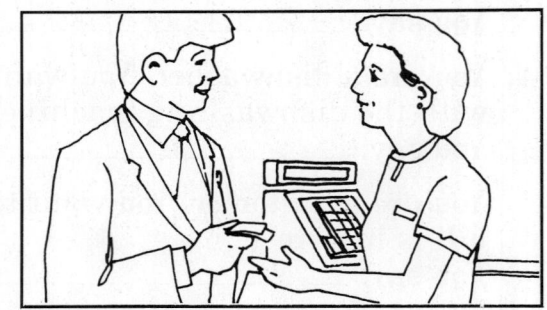

6. cashier

Duties

___ takes orders

___ clears tables

___ washes dishes

___ serves water

___ sets tables

___ writes up bills

___ cooks food

___ receives money

___ stocks kitchen

___ empties dishwashing machine

TALKING TOGETHER

Today's Specials
Hamburger and fries $5.95
Fish and chips $4.95
Beef stew and mashed potatoes $8.95
Egg salad sandwich $2.95
Vegetable soup $3.95
Chef's salad $4.95
Apple pie $2.50
Chocolate cake $2.00

In groups of 3-5 students, act out a scene in a restaurant.
In each group,
1 student is the waiter or waitress,
1 student is the cook,
and the rest are customers.

Complete the following steps:

1. The waiter or waitress asks for and writes the customers' orders. Ask the customers to repeat if you don't understand.

2. The waiter or waitress asks each customer if there is anything else he or she would like to order.

3. The waiter or waitress gives the orders to the cook. The cook reads the orders to the waiter or waitress. The waiter or waitress can also read the orders to the cook, who repeats the orders.

4. The waiter or waitress says what each customer ordered.

WORDS FOR WORK

Fill in the blanks with words from the box.

thanks	bread	quickly
water	enough	well done
hamburger	medium	cook
serves	clears	busboy
more	bill	customer

The _**customer**_ orders a _____ from Rosa. The _____ pours
       1   2   3

the _____ and brings the _____. Rosa _____ the busboy
     4   5   6

because he works _____. When Rosa _____ the customer his
                         7   8

hamburger, he says it isn't cooked _____. He wants it _____,
                                          9   10

but it's _____. The _____ cooks it a little _____. After the
       11   12   13

customer finishes eating, Rosa brings the _____ and the busboy
                                                          14

_____ the table.
   15

PARTNER WORK

Person 1

Speak to a partner. Choose one of the sentences (a, b, or c) from part 1. Your partner will respond with one of the sentences from part 1 on page 118. You respond with a sentence from part 2. Continue until the exercise is complete.

1. a. Can you help me?
   b. Hi. How's it going?
   c. Are there more clean glasses in the kitchen?

2. a. I can't find them.
   b. What's wrong?
   c. Please clear table four.

3. a. I'll cook another hamburger right away.
   b. Yes. The customers at table seven want more coffee.
   c. I see. Are these glasses dry?

4. a. You're welcome.
   b. Thank you very much.
   c. Can you unload them as soon as they're dry?

PARTNER WORK

Person 2

Your partner will say something to you. Choose an answer from part 1 (a, b, or c). Respond to the next thing your partner says with a sentence from part 2. Your partner's part is on page 117.

1. **a.** Sure. What do you need?
   b. Yes, over there.
   c. Not so great. There's a problem.

2. **a.** OK. Anything else?
   b. This hamburger is well done. The customer wanted it medium.
   c. Oh. The clean glasses are in the dishwasher.

3. **a.** OK. I'll serve the coffee right away.
   b. No, they aren't.
   c. Thank you!

4. **a.** I appreciate your help.
   b. Sure, I can.
   c. No problem.

STRUCTURE WORK

Part 1

Choose the correct contraction from the list below.

they're	couldn't
doesn't	you're
I'll	don't
what's	

1. Please unload the glasses as soon as _____ dry.
2. The dishwasher _____ work.
3. I _____ have enough silverware.
4. _____ cook the hamburger a little longer.
5. She _____ find enough glasses.
6. _____ welcome.
7. _____ the problem?

Part 2

Choose the correct word from the list below.

right	behind
more	longer
enough	quickly
well done	

1. The glasses are _____ the cups.
2. They don't have _____ bread. They need more.
3. She doesn't have the _____ coffee pot.
4. Please unload some _____ glasses.
5. She wants her hamburger _____.
6. That busboy serves coffee _____.
7. You need to cook the hamburger _____ to make it well done.

PROBLEM SOLVING

Can You Show Me How?

Read the conversations. Then act them out.

A: Can you show me how to put soap in the dishwasher?

B: I don't have time for anyone else's work. I have enough of my own.

A: Fine. Just forget it.

A: Can you show me how to set the table?

B: What? I can't understand you. Ask someone else to help you. I'm busy.

A: Sorry to bother you.

- Are speakers A or B rude in either of the conversations?
- How do you answer someone who is rude?
- What can you say when someone helps you?

What Can You Say?

Finish the conversations.

1. **A:** Excuse me. Can you help me read this order?
   B: No, I can't. I'm too busy.
   A: _____

2. **A:** Can you show me how to turn on the dishwasher?
   B: Just a minute, please.
   A: _____

3. **A:** Can you help me carry these glasses?
   B: No, I don't have time.
   A: _____

4. **A:** Can you show me how to make coffee?
   B: Sure.
   A: _____

Chapter 11
Apologizing

I MISSED THE BUS

Look and Listen

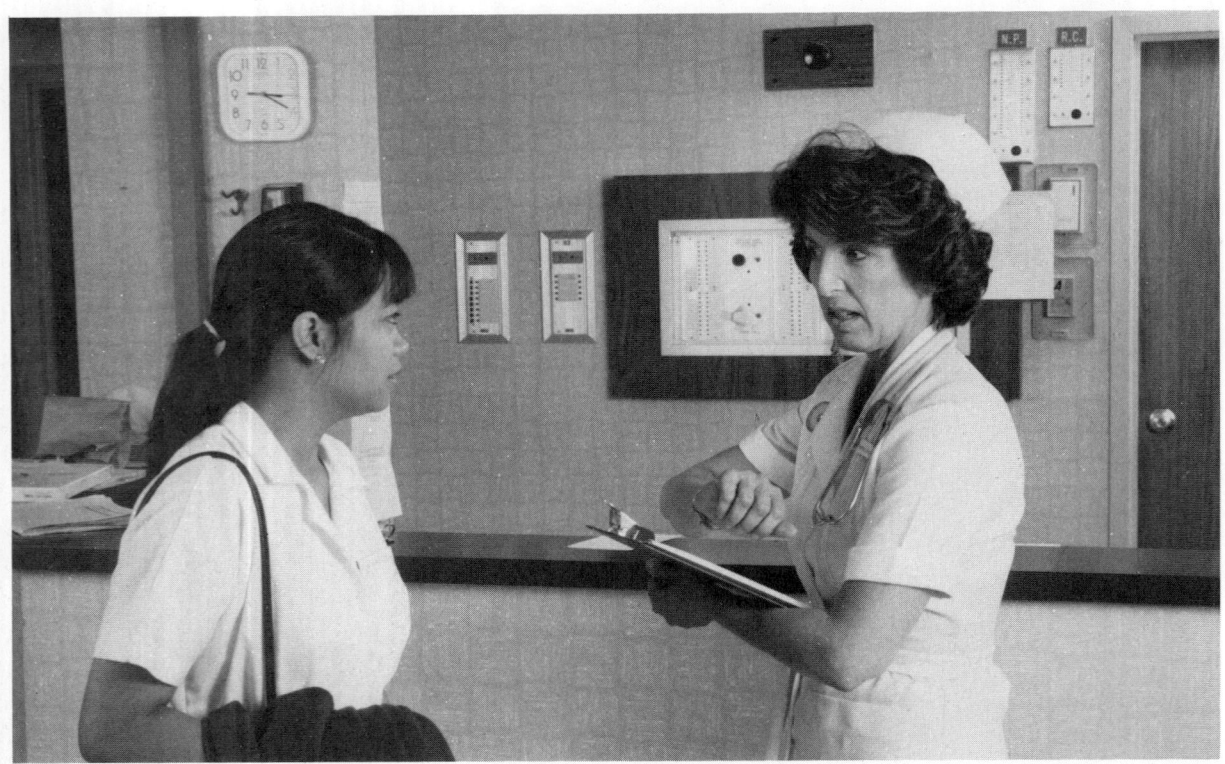

Mei: I'm sorry I'm late, Ms. Pappas. I missed the bus.

Ms. Pappas: Your shift begins at 3:00. You need to get to work on time.

Mei: I know. I'm sorry.

Ms. Pappas: Next time please try to call.

Mei: Maybe I should take an earlier bus.

Ms. Pappas: That's a good idea.

Check Your Understanding

Answer with Yes or No.

____ 1. Mei's shift begins at 3:00.

____ 2. Ms. Pappas wants Mei to work late.

____ 3. Mei says she missed the bus.

____ 4. Mei is talking to her boss.

____ 5. Ms. Pappas wants Mei to call home if she is late.

____ 6. It's OK if Mei is late for work.

Practice

Choose the missing statement or response from the box below, or make up your own. Practice speaking with a partner.

> Yes, I know. I'm sorry. It won't happen again.
> OK, I will, Ms. Pappas.
> I'm sorry. I missed my bus.

1. **Boss:** If you're going to be late, you need to call me right away.

   Worker: _____

2. **Boss:** It's important that you come to work on time.

   Worker: _____

3. **Boss:** Your shift begins at 3:00. You're late.

   Worker: _____

WE'RE SHORTHANDED TODAY

Look and Listen

Ms. Pappas: Why didn't you bathe the patient in Room 202?

Mei: We're shorthanded today.

Ms. Pappas: Can't another aide help you?

Mei: Everyone is very busy today. Two aides are out sick.

Ms. Pappas: I see. Let's do it right now.

Mei: Oh, thank you! I really appreciate it.

> - How does Mei feel?
> - Do you ever feel like this at work? Why?
> - Should Mei say, "I'm sorry"? Why or why not?

Practice

Choose an apology from the box below. Practice with a partner. Then practice each conversation making up your own responses.

> I'm sorry. Please show me what to do.
> I'm sorry. There was an accident on the freeway.
> Sorry. I'll come back later.
> Sorry. I ran out of sheets.
> I'm sorry. I've been too busy.
> I'm sorry. I forgot. I'll do it right now.
> I'm sorry. I didn't know where to put it.
> Oh, sorry. I didn't see the sign.

1. **A:** You're late.
   B: _____
2. **A:** Why didn't you give this patient her dinner?
   B: _____
3. **A:** Why didn't you change all the sheets?
   B: _____
4. **A:** Can't you see I'm busy right now?
   B: _____
5. **A:** Why didn't you punch the time clock?
   B: _____
6. **A:** Stop! Be careful or you'll break the machine.
   B: _____
7. **A:** Why didn't you put the medication in the cabinet?
   B: _____
8. **A:** This is a no-smoking area.
   B: _____

VOCABULARY

Match each sentence with the correct picture.

1.

2.

3.

4.

5.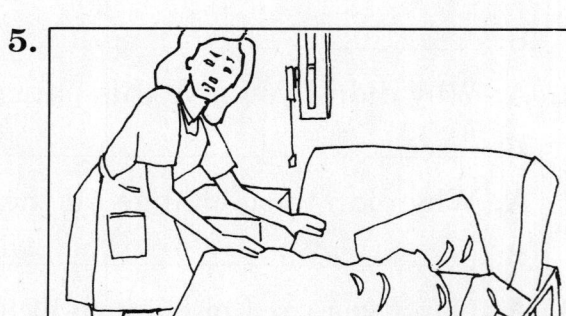

6.

____ She didn't know what to do.

____ He put the medications in the cabinet.

____ She missed the bus.

____ He punched in.

____ She came late.

____ He ran out of toilet paper.

TALKING TOGETHER

1. **Complete the following conversation. Then practice with a partner.**

   Boss: You didn't come to work yesterday and you didn't call.

   Worker: I'm sorry. I didn't know I had to call.

   Boss: Next time, please call and leave a message.

   Worker: _____

2. **Read about the situation and answer the questions. Put a check (✓) by the best response.**

   A worker breaks a machine. No one sees him. What should the worker do?

   ____ tell a coworker

   ____ tell his boss

   ____ say nothing

   The boss finds the broken machine. He asks, "Who did this?" What should the worker do?

   ____ say he broke the machine

   ____ say a coworker broke the machine

   ____ say nothing

WORDS FOR WORK

Fill in the blanks below with the correct words from this list.

sorry	apologized
important	late
call	gets
on time	begins

Mei's shift __begins__ at 3:00. Today she was _____ because she
                  1   2
missed the bus. Usually she _____ to work _____. She
                              3   4
_____ to her boss when she got to work. It's _____ to come
   5   6
to work on time. Her boss said that if Mei is late, she needs to
_____. Mei said she was _____ she came to work late.
    7   8

WATCH OUT!

Look at the picture and read the conversation.

Mei: Hey! Watch out!

Zosia: I'm sorry. I didn't see you.

Mei: You shouldn't walk so fast!

Zosia: I'm really sorry. Are you OK?

Mei: Yes, I'm fine.

Zosia: Here, I'll pick that up for you.

Mei: Thank you.

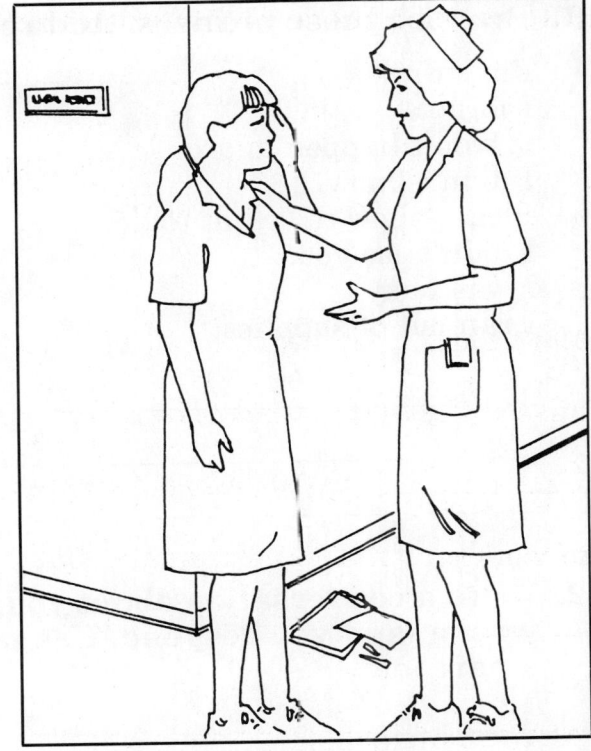

Answer the questions. Work with a group.

1. Why does Mei say, "Watch out!"?
2. Does Zosia say, "I'm sorry"? Does she give a reason?
3. How does Zosia help Mei?
4. Have you ever had an accident at work? What happened? What did you say?

SPEAKING PRACTICE

1. **Practice these phrases. Add reasons to the list.**

   I'm sorry.
   I forgot.
   It won't happen again.
   I didn't know.
   Please show me what to do.
   I didn't see you.
   I was busy.
   I ran out of supplies.

   _____

   _____

2. **Write a conversation about your job. The boss tells what you did wrong, and you respond. Use phrases from the list. Practice with a partner.**

   Your boss: _____

   _____

   You: _____

   _____

   Your boss: _____

   _____

   You: _____

   _____

   Your boss: _____

   _____

   You: _____

   _____

STRUCTURE WORK

Part 1

The past tense of most verbs is formed by adding *-ed*.

Example:	Present Tense	Past Tense
paint	paint**ed**
walk	walk**ed**
laugh	laugh**ed**

Write the past tense of the regular verbs in parentheses.

1. Mei __missed__ her bus.
   (miss)

2. Zosia just _____ with the patient.
   (talk)

3. Enrique _____ in sick.
   (call)

4. She _____ her boss for a raise.
   (ask)

Part 2

Study the verb chart to review some irregular verbs. Then, in the blanks, write the past tense of the irregular verbs in parentheses.

Present	Past
break	broke
give	gave
have	had
say, says	said
wake	woke

5. I think you _____ the (break) machine.

6. Yesterday I _____ to (have) help Ms. Pappas.

7. He was late because he _____ up late. (wake)

8. Mele _____ the patient (give) her medication 15 minutes ago.

9. The patient _____ she (say) needed pain relief.

PROBLEM SOLVING

What Should They Say?

Decide what the people are saying. Then act out the situations.

1.

2.

The Missing Medications

Complete the conversation. Think about the discussion questions below. Then act out the conversation with a partner.

Some medications are missing from the storage room. Stefano was in the storage room yesterday, but he didn't take the medications.

Boss: Do you know where those medications are?

Stefano: No, I don't.

Boss: You were in the storage room yesterday.

Stefano: I don't know anything about them. Can I help you find them?

Boss: We need to find out who took them.

Stefano: Maybe they are in the other storage room.

Boss: Well, I want them back here by tomorrow morning.

Stefano: _____

- Does Stefano's boss think Stefano is telling the truth?
- How does Stefano feel? What does he say? Why?
- What do you do when your boss treats you unfairly?

Chapter 12
Requesting Location

HOW DO I GET TO THE BUSINESS OFFICE?

Look and Listen

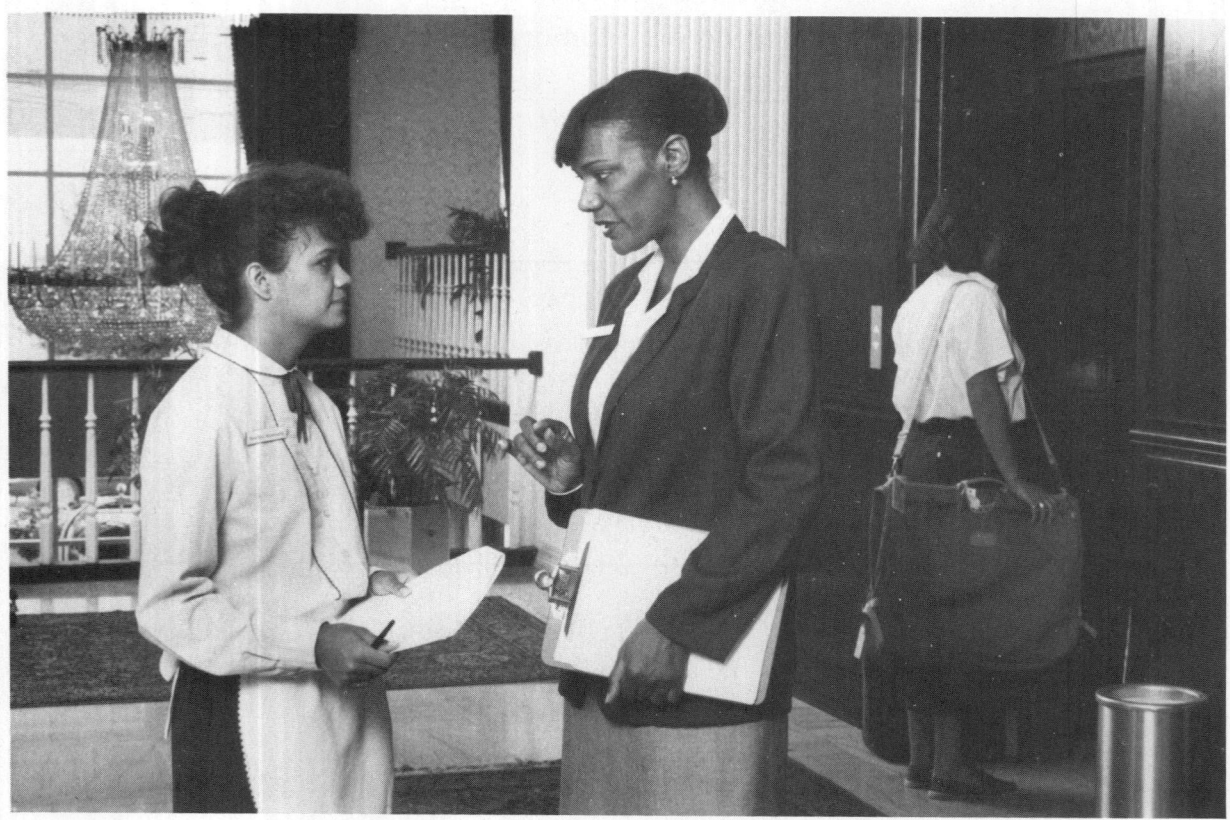

Maria: Excuse me. How do I get to the business office?

Ms. Smith: Go to the first floor. Turn left, go past the restaurant, and turn right. It's the first door. You can't miss it.

Maria: I'm sorry. Do I turn left or right after the restaurant?

Ms. Smith: Turn right. The business office is the first door on the left.

Maria: The first door on the left. I think I've got it. Thanks, Ms. Smith.

Check Your Understanding
Circle Yes or No.

1. Maria knows how to get to the business office.   Yes   No
2. The business office is downstairs.   Yes   No
3. Ms. Smith is going to take Maria to the business office.   Yes   No
4. Maria has to go upstairs.   Yes   No
5. The business office is the second door on the left.   Yes   No

---

- How does Maria ask for help?
- How does she show that she understands the directions?

Practice

Tell how to get to these places in your school. Practice with a partner.

A: How do I get to _____?

B: Go _____
_____.

the women's room/the men's room

the office

the front door

the second floor

the vending machines

IT'S STRAIGHT DOWN THE HALL

Look and Listen

Guest: Excuse me. I'm looking for the rest room.

Maria: It's straight down the hall. You turn right at the front desk.

Guest: Oh, I see. Over there across from the gift shop?

Maria: Yes, that's right.

Guest: Thank you very much.

Maria: No problem.

Practice

Look at the floor plan below. Ask a partner the questions that follow.

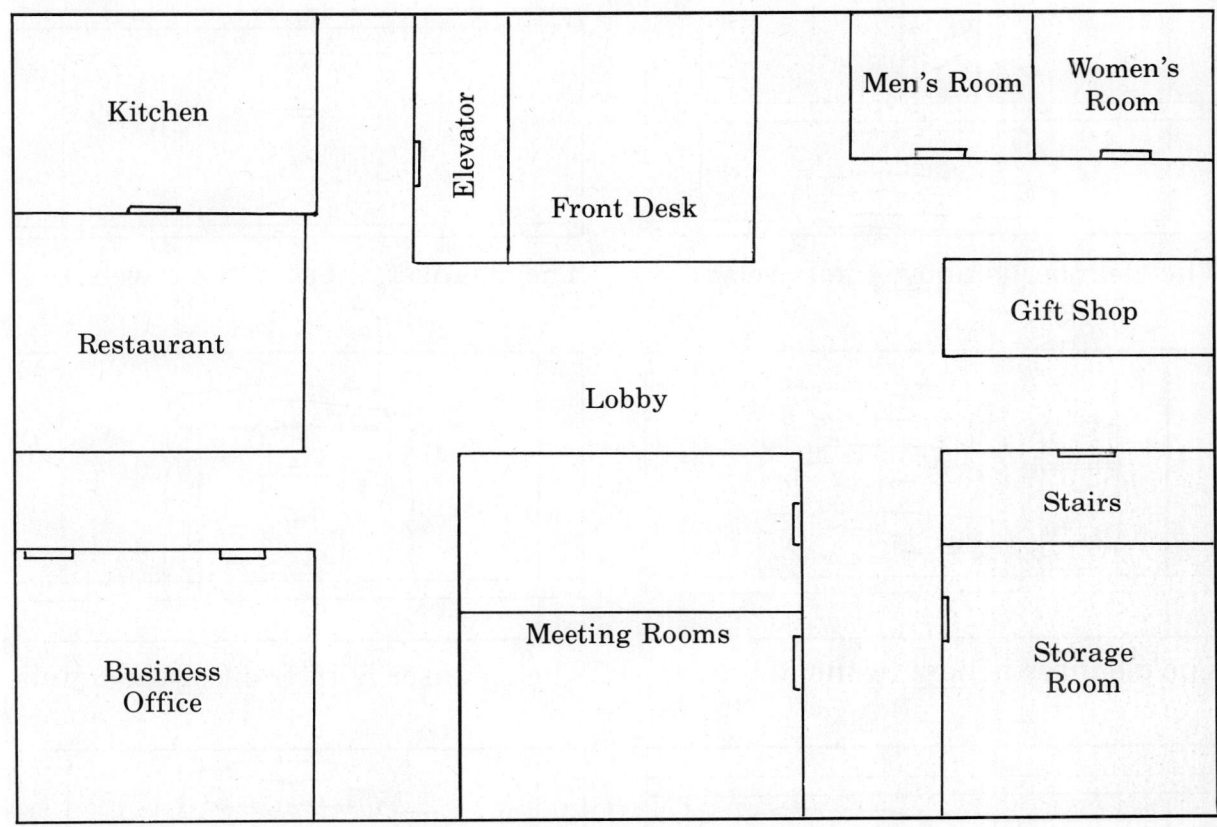

1. Excuse me. Where's the elevator?
2. Where's the women's room?
3. Where are the stairs?
4. Do you know where the meeting rooms are?
5. Where's the kitchen?
6. Do you know where the gift shop is?
7. How do I get to the storage room?
8. Excuse me. How do I get to the restaurant?
9. Where's the storage room?
10. Where is the business office?

VOCABULARY

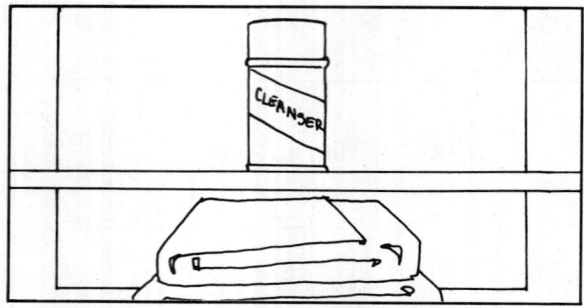
The cleanser is <u>above</u> the towels.

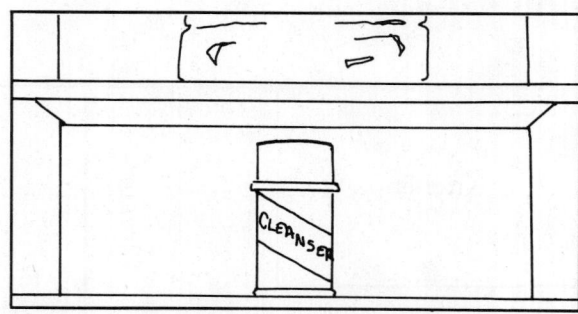
The cleanser is <u>below</u> the towels.

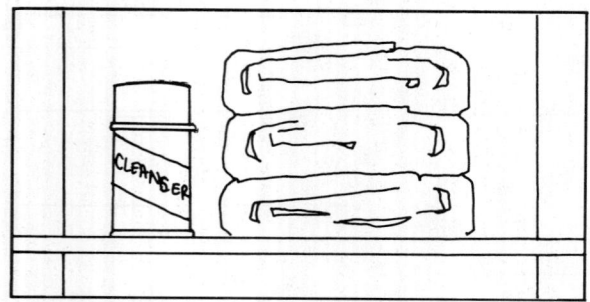
The cleanser is <u>next to</u> the towels.

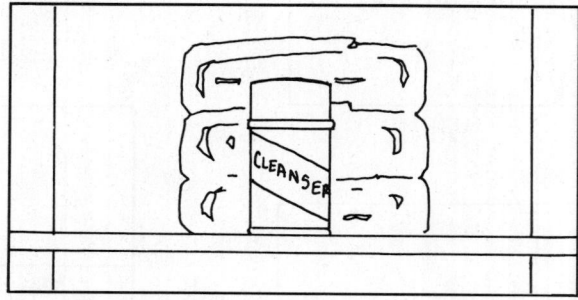
The cleanser is <u>in front of</u> the towels.

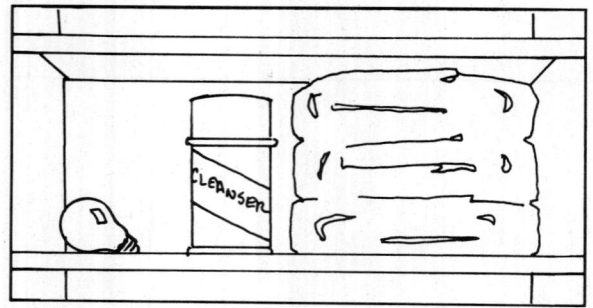
The cleanser is <u>between</u> the towels and the light bulb.

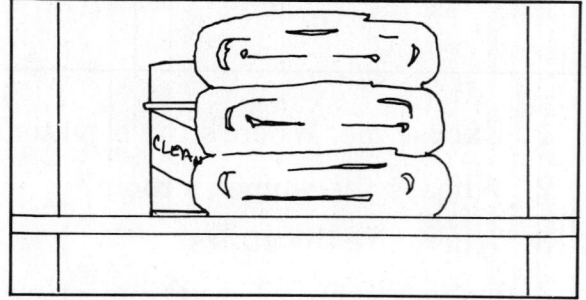
The cleanser is <u>behind</u> the towels.

TALKING TOGETHER

Look at the picture below and practice the following conversations with a partner.

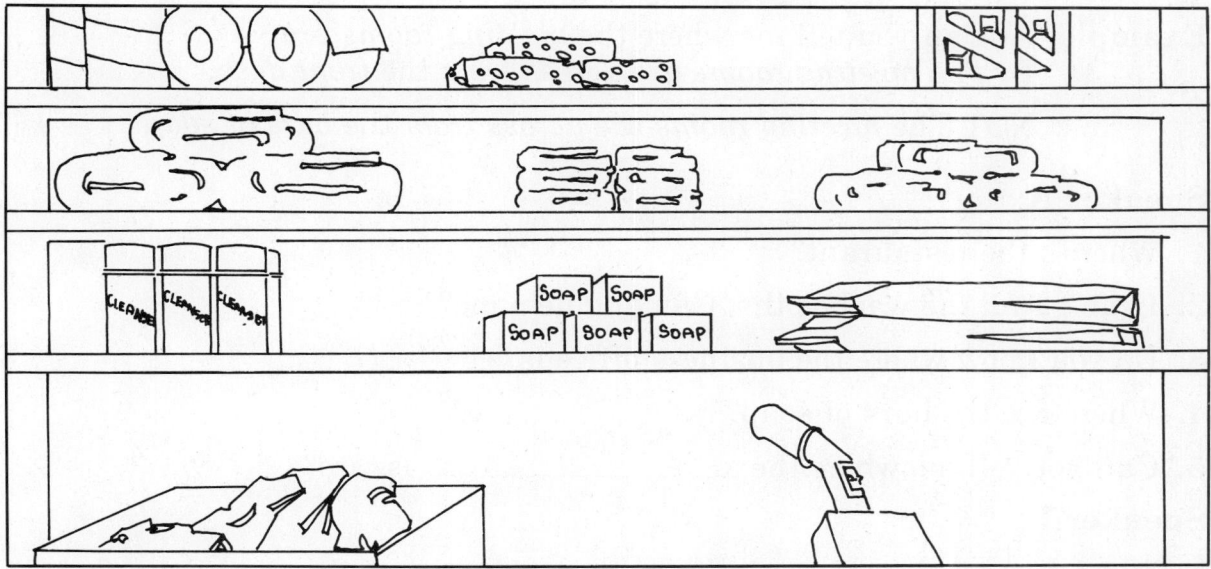

A: Can you tell me where the <u>cleanser</u> is?

B: It's <u>on the bottom shelf</u>.

A: I don't see it.

B: <u>On the bottom shelf next to the soap.</u>

A: Oh, I see it. Thanks.

A: Where are the <u>rags</u>?

B: They're <u>in a box below the cleanser</u>.

A: I don't see them.

B: <u>Below the cleanser next to the vacuum cleaner.</u>

A: Oh, there. Thanks.

Now substitute the underlined words above with the words below and complete the conversation correctly. Use the expressions in the box.

below	on the top shelf	to the left of
next to	on the middle shelf	to the right of
between	on the bottom shelf	

1. toilet paper
2. large towels
3. soap
4. vacuum cleaner

WORDS FOR WORK

Part 1

Speaker A asks the questions. Speaker B chooses logical answers from the choices below. Practice both parts.

Example: A: Can you tell me where the *meeting rooms* are?
B: The *meeting rooms* are *across from* the *front desk*.

NOT The *meeting rooms* are *across from* the *bars of soap*.

Speaker A:

1. Where's the restaurant?
2. I can't find the washcloths. Can you help me?
3. Do you know where the business office is?
4. Where are the bars of soap?
5. Can you tell me where the _____ is/are?

Speaker B:

The	large towels	is/are	across from	the	small towels
	restaurant		to the left of		gift shop
	elevator		next to		front desk
	business office		to the right of		cleanser
	bars of soap		behind		kitchen
	washcloths		below		bars of soap
	meeting rooms		above		sponges

Part 2

Which word does *not* belong? Cross it out.

1. sponges   light bulbs   ~~storage room~~   cleanser
2. to the left   kitchen   across from   below
3. front desk   restaurant   women's room   bars of soap
4. stairs   rags   toilet paper   vacuum cleaner
5. next to   elevator   above   behind

SPEAKING PRACTICE

Look at the picture below. Read both parts of each conversation and fill in the answers. Then practice with a partner.

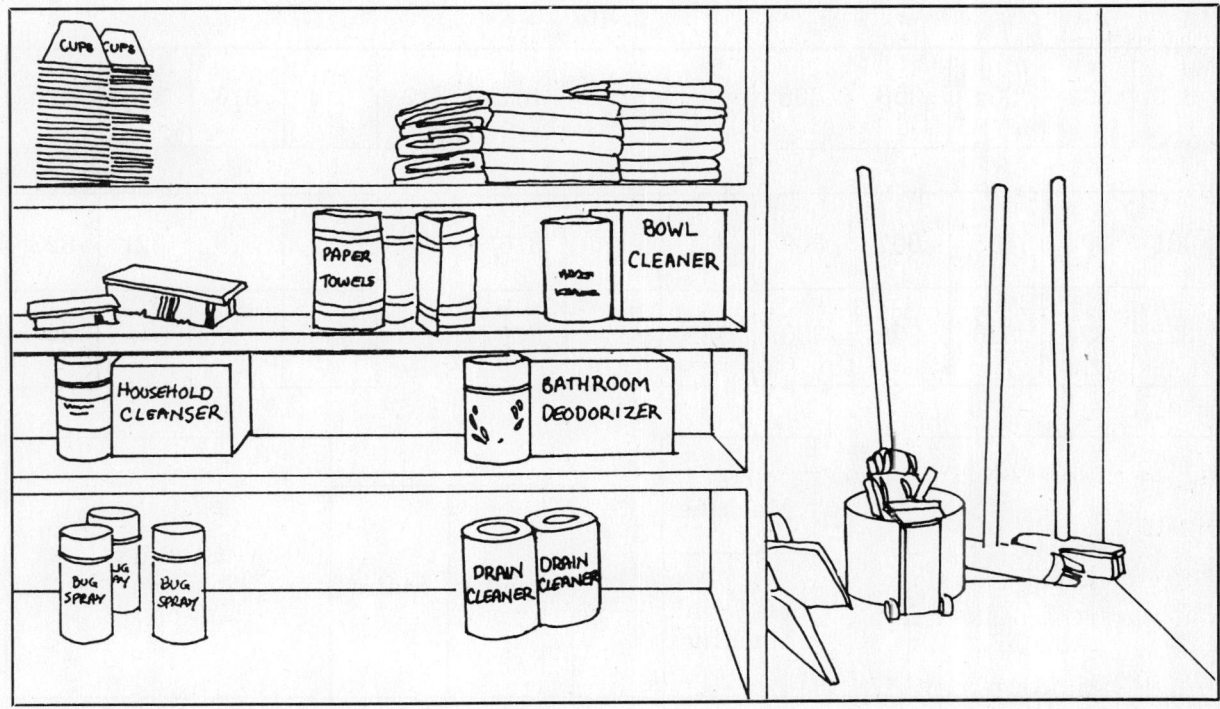

1. I ran out of _____.

   It's on the second shelf on the far right.

2. Where's the _____?

   It's on the floor, below the household cleanser.

3. I need a _____. Is there one here?

   Yes, in the closet to the right of the mops.

4. Are there any _____ in here?

   Yes, on the top shelf to the left of the sheets.

5. I need some _____.

   They're on the middle shelf between the brushes and the bowl cleaner.

6. Where are the _____?

   They're on the top shelf next to the plastic cups.

SPEAKING PRACTICE

Look at the hotel floor plan below. Have a partner read you the directions. Start from the storage room each time. Answer the questions.

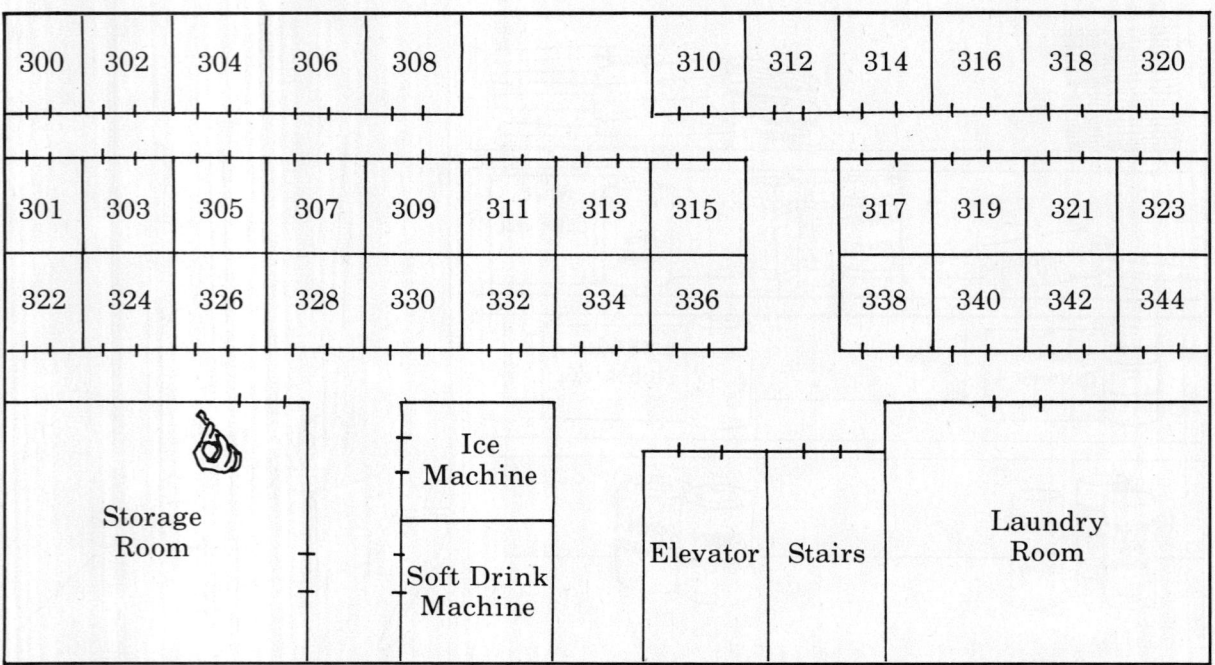

1. Turn right. Go to the end of the hall. It's the last door on the right.

   Where are you?

2. Turn left. Go down the hall. It's the second door on the right.

   Where are you?

3. Turn right. Go down the hall. At Room 336, turn left. Turn left again and go down the hallway. It's the fifth door on the left side.

   Where are you?

4. Turn right. Turn right again down the first hall. It's next to the ice machine.

   Where are you?

5. Turn right. Go down the hall. They're between the elevator and the laundry room.

   Where are you?

STRUCTURE WORK

Finish each sentence using the correct contraction. Choose from the list below.

I'm	it's
you're	we're
he's	you're
she's	they're

1. Where's the elevator?
   _____ next to the stairs.

2. Where's Ms. Smith?
   _____ in the storage room.

3. Where are the brushes?
   _____ next to the paper towels.

4. Where's Mr. Boone?
   _____ in Room 309.

5. I'm lost. Where am I?
   _____ in the laundry room.

6. Where are Ms. Smith and Maria?
   _____ on the second floor next to the elevators.

7. Where's the men's room?
   _____ straight down the hall.

8. Hey, Maria! Where are you?
   _____ over here.

9. How do I get to the front desk?
   _____ in the lobby, on the first floor.

10. Can you tell me where the soap is?
    _____ next to the cleanser.

PROBLEM SOLVING

Where Is It?

Role-play the following parts. Practice both parts.

1. **A.** Ask another student where the business office is at your school.
   B. Give directions.

2. **A.** Ask another student how to go from the parking area or the front door at your school to the classroom.
   B. Give directions.

3. **A.** Ask another student where something you need is in the classroom.
   B. Give directions.

4. **A.** Ask another student where something is in your school.
   B. Give directions.

Talk About It

Discuss these questions.

1. Do you feel comfortable asking someone you don't know for directions?
2. What can help you remember complicated directions?
3. Do people ever ask you for directions? What happens?

What Should Maria Do?

Circle the letter of the answer you think is best. Give a reason for your answer.

1. Maria needs to see the manager now. She thinks she knows how to get to the manager's office, but she's not sure. What should she do?
   a. Try to find her own way
   b. Ask another worker for directions
   c. Look for the manager tomorrow

2. She gets directions to the lunchroom from a coworker, but she gets lost. What should she do?
   a. Try to find someone she knows to ask for directions
   b. Ask anyone for directions
   c. Eat lunch in another place

3. She runs out of cleanser, and there is none in the storage room. There may be some in another storage room, but she doesn't know where it is. What should she do?
   a. Do her job without cleanser
   b. Ask anyone for directions to the other storage room
   c. Find her supervisor and ask for help

4. She needs help lifting some heavy supplies. No one is in the storage room to help her. What should she do?
   a. Try to lift the supplies herself
   b. Look for her supervisor to get help
   c. Find a coworker and ask for help

Chapter 13
Observing Safety

YOU NEED TO WEAR YOUR HARD HAT

Look and Listen

Ming: Felipe, you need to wear your hard hat in this area. You could get hurt.

Felipe: I'm sorry. I forgot. I'm new at this.

Ming: Did you see the sign?

Felipe: No, I didn't.

Ming: Look, it's over there. You could lose your job if you don't wear a hard hat here.

Felipe: I'll be more careful. Thanks.

Check Your Understanding

Circle Yes or No.

1. Felipe and Ming are coworkers. Yes No
2. Ming is wearing a hard hat. Yes No
3. Everyone in the area must wear a hard hat. Yes No
4. Felipe saw the sign. Yes No
5. Ming wants to help Felipe. Yes No
6. Felipe is glad Ming talked to him. Yes No

- Is it OK for Ming to talk to a coworker this way?
- Why does Felipe say, "Thanks"?

Practice

Put the words below in the correct sentences. Practice the conversation with a partner.

careful	wear
hard hat	forgot
lose	sign

Ming: Hey! Where is your _____ ?
                                                1

Felipe: Oh. I _____ to bring it. I didn't see the _____
                      2   3
over there.

Ming: You know you could _____ your job if you don't
                                                    4
_____ your hard hat.
       5

Felipe: You're right. Thanks for reminding me. I'll be more
_____ .
       6

WATCH HOW I'M PUTTING ON THIS MASK

Look and Listen

Mr. Carter: Felipe, watch how I'm putting on this mask.

Ming: It has to fit tight against your face.

Juan: I got sick when I didn't wear my mask.

Felipe: Do I have to wear this mask all the time?

Mr. Carter: No. Ming will give you the safety equipment you need each day.

Ming: But always look for signs that warn of danger.

- Do you need safety equipment for your job?
- At your job, are there "Danger" signs? Where?

Practice

Fill in the blanks with the words below.

| turn off | ear plugs | hard hat |
| safety glasses | put on | respirator |

1. What should he do? He should put on a _____.

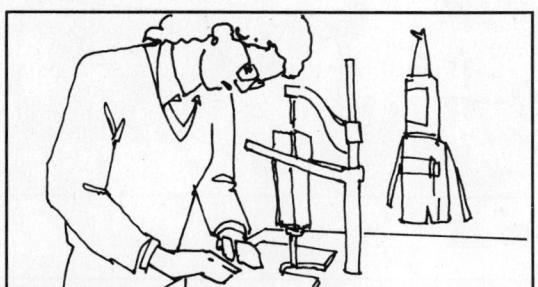

2. What should she do? She should _____ her apron.

3. What should he do? He should _____ the machine.

4. What should he do? He should put on a _____.

5. What should she do? She should wear _____.

6. What should he do? He should put on his _____.

VOCABULARY

Write the word or words from the box under each picture.

> safety glasses   apron
> safety gloves   face shield
> work boots   respirator
> ear plugs   dust mask

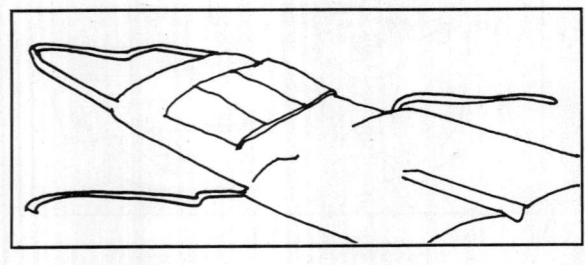

1. _____

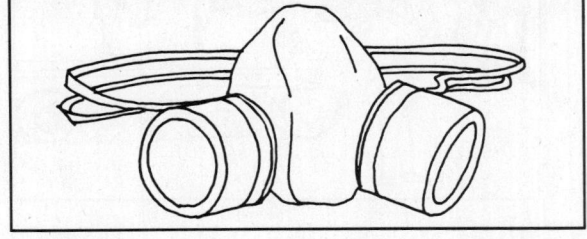

5. _____

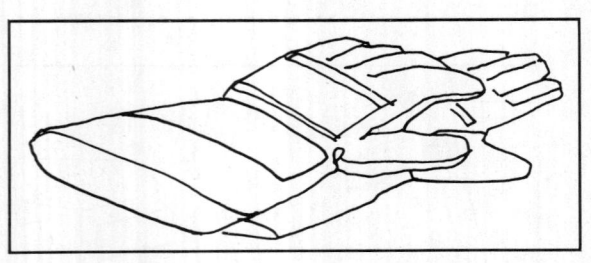

2. _____

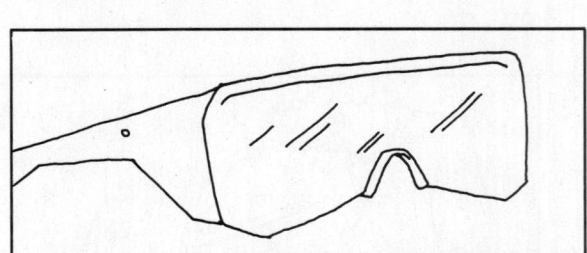

6. _____

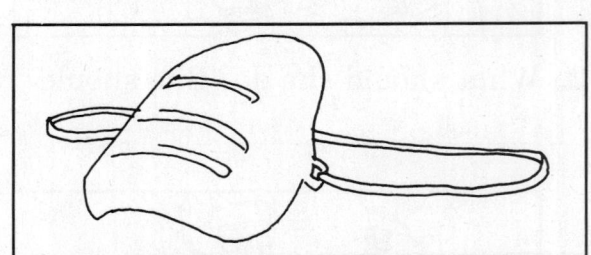

7. _____

3. _____

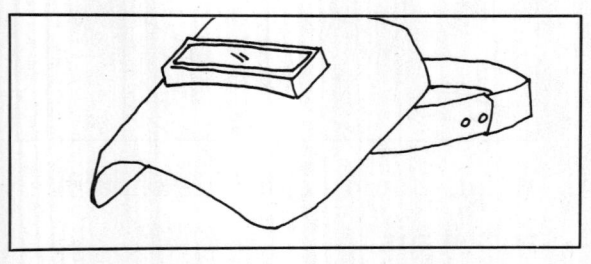

4. _____

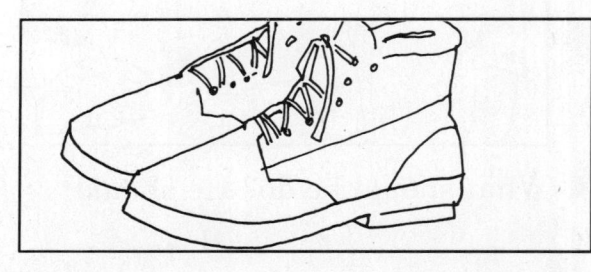

8. _____

TALKING TOGETHER

Role-play the following parts. Practice both parts.

1. **A:** You see a new worker not wearing her hard hat. You remind her to wear it.

   B: You say you forgot to put it on.

2. **A:** You tell a coworker he could lose his job if he doesn't wear gloves and safety glasses.

   B: You thank your coworker for telling you.

3. **A:** You tell a coworker she may get hurt if she doesn't wear a face shield.

   B: You promise to be more careful.

4. **A:** You look up from your machine to say hello to a coworker. You do not turn off the machine.

   B: Your coworker asks you to turn off the machine when you're not looking at it.

WORDS FOR WORK

Choose a word or group of words from each list to form a command. Write as many commands as you can. Remember to begin each command with a capital letter.

Example: don't forget   your safety glasses
Don't forget your safety glasses.

List 1	List 2
turn off	your ear plugs
don't leave on	the machine
put on	your safety glasses
don't forget	a face shield
wear	the respirator
	your gloves
	an apron
	a dust mask

1. _____
2. _____
3. _____
4. _____
5. _____
6. _____
7. _____
8. _____
9. _____
10. _____

Write a command for your job.
_____

SPEAKING PRACTICE

Part 1

Practice the conversation with a partner.

A: This is your work station. Your must observe safety at all times.

B: OK.

A: You need to wear work boots and a face shield while you're working.

B: OK, I've got it. Work boots and a face shield.

A: Yes. You must protect your feet and face.

Part 2

Practice the conversation with a partner. Use words from the box.

safety glasses	hands
ear plugs	feet
work boots	face
gloves	clothes
an apron	lungs
a respirator	ears
a face shield	
a dust mask	

A: This is your work station. You must observe safety at all times.

B: OK.

A: You need to wear _____ and _____ while you're working.

B: OK, I've got it. _____ and _____.

A: Yes. You must protect your _____ and _____.

SPEAKING PRACTICE

Work with a partner. Write the correct letter(s) under each sign.

A. Walk carefully.
B. Use this door only in an emergency.
C. There's an electrical current.
D. Do not go in. Stay away.
E. Go slowly here.
F. Do not smoke or light a match here.
G. Watch out! There's a dog.
H. Use this in case of fire.

FIRE ALARM	DANGER HIGH VOLTAGE
1. _____	5. _____
KEEP OUT	BEWARE OF DOG
2. _____	6. _____
EMERGENCY EXIT	FLAMMABLE
3. _____	7. _____
CAUTION	WATCH YOUR STEP
4. _____	8. _____

NEW EXPRESSIONS

Make commands from the following descriptions. The expressions in the box may help you.

Example: You want to warn a coworker to put on his hard hat.
You say: *Don't forget to put on your hard hat.*

> Watch out!
> Stop! Don't _____!
> Be careful!
> Watch your step!
> You'd better . . .
> Don't forget to . . .

1. You want to warn a coworker about some water on the floor.

    You say: _____

2. A coworker forgot to put on his safety glasses. You want to warn him.

    You say: _____

3. A coworker is smoking near a sign that says FLAMMABLE. You want to tell him to stop.

    You say: _____

4. Someone is going to go out the emergency exit. You want to stop her.

    You say: _____

5. You want to tell a coworker to put on gloves because it's a company safety rule.

    You say: _____

6. You want to tell a coworker not to look out the window or the boss will get mad.

    You say: _____

PROBLEM SOLVING

Safe or Unsafe?

Read the safety rules.

> **Safety Rules**
> 1. Always pay attention to your work.
> 2. Wear a hard hat in designated areas.
> 3. Always wear work boots with rubber soles.
> 4. Wipe up any spills immediately.
> 5. Always wear safety glasses when you operate machinery.
> 6. Keep the floor of your work station clean.
> 7. Do not take medicine that causes drowsiness.
> 8. After work, put all equipment away and turn off power.
> 9. Never run in the production area.
> 10. Never drink alcohol at work or before work.

Read each situation. Circle Safe or Unsafe.

1. Juan is late. He's running to his work station.   Safe   Unsafe
2. Paul is wearing safety glasses at the drilling machine.   Safe   Unsafe
3. Maria has a cold. She is taking medication that makes her sleepy.   Safe   Unsafe
4. Aruna is wearing work boots with leather soles.   Safe   Unsafe
5. Ming is wearing a hard hat in the hard-hat area.   Safe   Unsafe
6. Mayumi leaves some equipment out after work.   Safe   Unsafe

Do you know the safety rules at your job? What are some of them?

Safety Problems

Look at the following pictures. List the safety problems. Then tell what you would say to the worker. If there are no problems, write Safe.

1. Problems: _____

3. Problems: _____

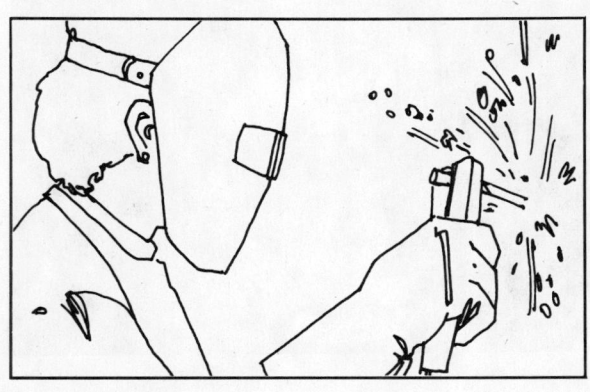

2. Problems: _____

4. Problems: _____

- Do you report unsafe situations at work? If so, give examples.
- Do you warn coworkers of danger?

Chapter 14
Work Schedule Changes

CAN I CHANGE MY SCHEDULE?

Look and Listen

Juan: Mr. Carter, could I talk to you for a minute?

Mr. Carter: Sure. What's on your mind?

Juan: I need to change my work schedule from the late shift to the early shift.

Mr. Carter: Why?

Juan: I want to take some classes in the evening.

Mr. Carter: Well, I'll see what I can do.

Juan: When will you know?

Mr. Carter: Come see me on Monday afternoon.

Juan: OK. Thank you, Mr. Carter.

Check Your Understanding
Circle Yes or No.

1. Mr. Carter is Juan's supervisor.   Yes   No
2. Juan wants to work the late shift.   Yes   No
3. Juan wants to change his schedule so he can work a second job.   Yes   No
4. Mr. Carter says he will change the work schedule.   Yes   No
5. Juan wants to take evening classes.   Yes   No
6. Mr. Carter tells Juan to come back on Monday morning.   Yes   No

---

- At your job, can you change your schedule?
- Who do you talk to?

Practice

1. What are some good reasons to ask for a schedule change? List them:

   _____

   _____

2. Practice the conversation with a partner. Use one of the reasons above.

   You: Can I change my schedule from _____ to _____?

   Supervisor: I'm not sure. Why?

   You: Well, _____.

I WANT TO TAKE ONE WEEK OF VACATION

Look and Listen

Ming: Mr. Carter, could I talk to you about taking a vacation?

Mr. Carter: Sure.

Ming: I'd like to take a week off in April.

Mr. Carter: Did you fill out a vacation request form?

Ming: Not yet.

Mr. Carter: OK. Fill out this form. Write your name here and the dates you want off.

Ming: When will I find out?

Mr. Carter: I'll let you know next week.

Ming: OK. Thanks.

Practice

Practice with a partner. Speaker A asks a question. Speaker B chooses the best answer and tells Speaker A.

1. **A:** I want to change my work schedule. What should I do?
   B: a. Tell your supervisor to make the change.
      b. Ask your supervisor if you can make a change.

2. **A:** I'm finished filling out my vacation request form. What should I do?
   B: a. Return it to your supervisor two weeks before your vacation.
      b. Return it to your supervisor now.

3. **A:** I asked my supervisor to make a schedule change. He said no. What should I do?
   B: a. Explain to your supervisor why the change is important.
      b. Ask another supervisor to make the change.

4. **A:** I returned my vacation request form three weeks ago. I have no answer. What should I do?
   B: a. Go back to your supervisor and ask for an answer.
      b. Wait another week. Then ask your supervisor for an answer.

5. **A:** I want Saturday off this week. What should I do?
   B: a. Find a coworker to take your place and ask the supervisor.
      b. Don't bother your supervisor. She's very busy.

- Do you get vacation time at your job? How much?
- At your job, how do you ask for a vacation?

VOCABULARY

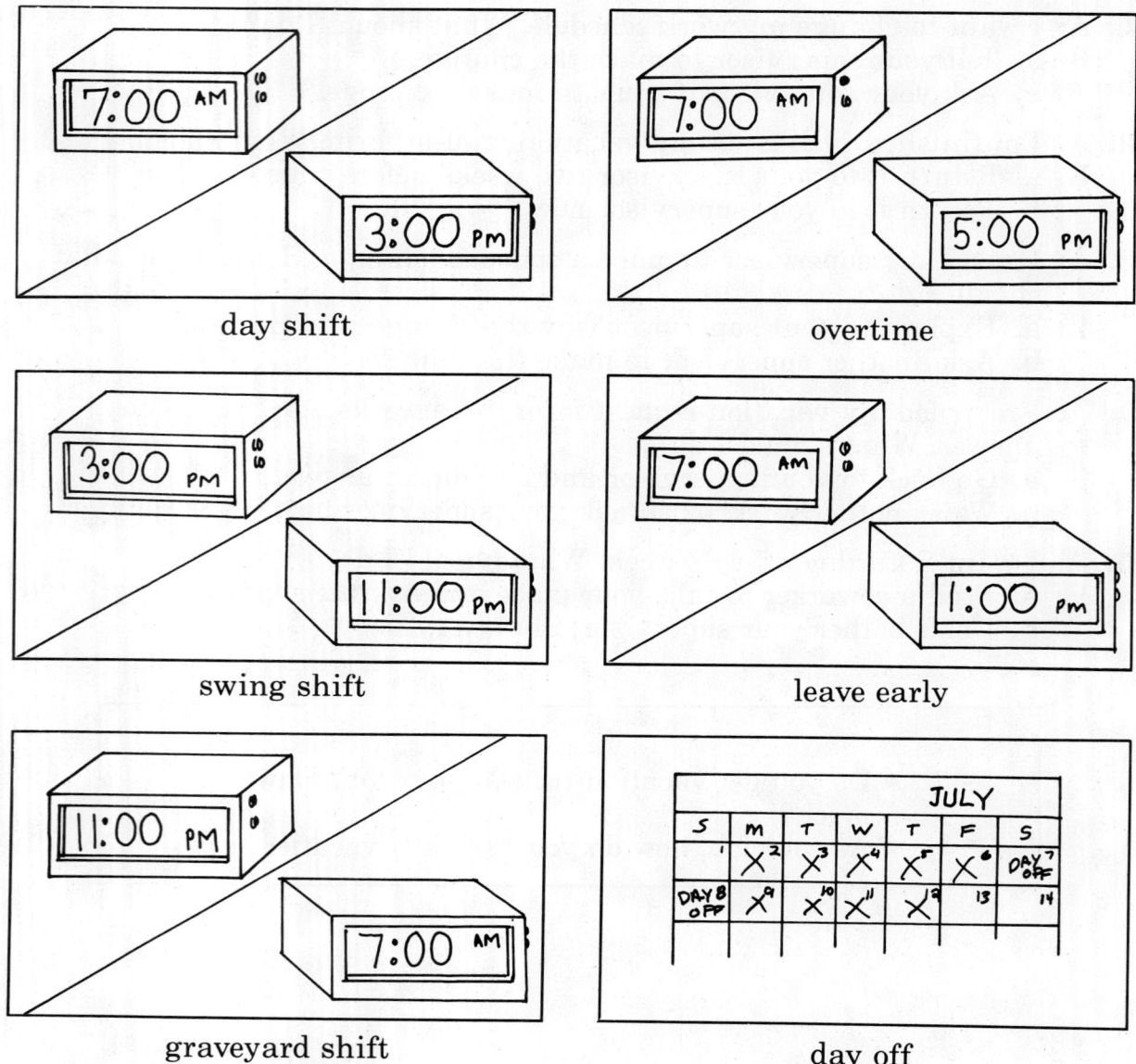

day shift

overtime

swing shift

leave early

graveyard shift
night shift

day off

Answer the questions.
1. What shift do you work?
2. Do you often work overtime?
3. Do you often leave early?
4. What are your days off?

TALKING TOGETHER

Read the work schedule below. Then answer the questions. Work with a group.

Work Schedule—May 8-13 Day Shift—7 A.M.-3 P.M.					
Mon.	Tues.	Wed.	Thurs.	Fri.	Sat.
Juan	Juan	Juan	Paola	Paola	Juan
Ming	Aruna	Aruna	Ming	Ming	Aruna
Swing Shift—3 P.M.-11 P.M.					
Aruna	Ming	Ming	Juan	Juan	Ming
Paola	Paola	Paola	Aruna	Aruna	Paola

1. Is this schedule for May 8-13 or May 13-17?
2. When is the day shift? When is the swing shift?
3. What hours does Paola work on Thursday?
4. Which shift does Aruna work on Monday?
5. What time do Juan and Aruna begin work on Wednesday?
6. Who works with Ming on Tuesday?
7. How many days a week does each person work?
8. Does anyone work on weekends?
9. Does anyone work with the same coworkers every day?
10. How many hours a week does each person work?

WORDS FOR WORK

Read the paragraphs below and match the underlined words with their meanings. Then put each word in the correct list.

Victor works the swing shift—3 P.M. to 11 P.M. He works full-time on weekdays. Right now he needs money, so he likes to work overtime. Last week, he worked 62 hours.

Sometimes he works the graveyard shift and sleeps during the day. When he works weekends, too, he doesn't have a day off. In two months he wants to take a vacation. He wants to visit his family in Mexico. He's going to fill out a request form, sign it, and return it to his supervisor.

1. swing shift   ____ a day of no work
2. full-time   ____ late-night hours
3. weekdays   ____ Saturday and Sunday
4. overtime   ____ write your name
5. graveyard shift   ____ 40 hours a week
6. weekends   ____ a holiday from work
7. day off   ____ extra hours of work beyond 40
8. vacation   ____ write in the information
9. fill out   ____ Monday through Friday
10. sign   ____ afternoon and evening hours

Work times
swing shift
_____
_____
_____

Parts of the week
_____
_____

Time off
day off
_____

Actions
_____
_____

SPEAKING PRACTICE

Practice the conversations with a partner. Practice both parts. Then substitute your own information.

Supervisor: Juan, one of the swing-shift workers is sick. Can you work late?

Juan: How late do you want me to work?

Supervisor: I can use you until 6:00.

Juan: I'm sorry. What time did you say?

Supervisor: 6:00.

Juan: OK. I can work.

Supervisor: Thanks a lot for helping us out.

Juan: No problem.

Supervisor: Ming, one of the early-shift workers had a family emergency. Can you come in early tomorrow?

Ming: How early do you want me to come in?

Supervisor: Can you come in at 6:00?

Ming: I didn't get that. What time?

Supervisor: 6:00.

Ming: I'm sorry. I can't. I have an appointment at 8:00.

Supervisor: OK. Thanks, anyway.

- Does your supervisor ask you to work overtime?
- Do you get paid extra for working overtime?
- Does your supervisor ask you to come in early?

SPEAKING PRACTICE

Answer the questions.

1. What are some good reasons to give for *not* working overtime? List them:

   _____
   _____
   _____

2. Practice the conversations. Give your own reasons for not working late.

   Supervisor: Can you work late today?
   Worker: I'm sorry. I can't. I _____.
   Supervisor: Thanks, anyway.

   Supervisor: Can you come in early tomorrow?
   Worker: I'm sorry. I can't. I _____.
   Supervisor: Thanks, anyway.

3. What will happen if you often come in early or work overtime? What will happen if you often say you can't come in early or work overtime?

NEW EXPRESSIONS

For each statement, make a question. Use the expressions in the box. Follow the example.

> Could I please
> Could I possibly
>   Can I   take Saturday off?
>   May I
> Is it OK if I

1. I want to take Monday off.
   Is it OK if I take Monday off?

2. I want to work the late shift on Tuesday.

3. I want to work the early shift on Friday.

4. I want to take a vacation in April.

5. I want to change my schedule.

6. I want to work Wednesday instead of Thursday.

7. I want to come in early and leave early tomorrow.

8. I want to come in late on Tuesday.

PROBLEM SOLVING

Changing Your Schedule

Act out the conversations. Practice both parts.

1. **A:** Can I please change my work schedule?
   B: Why do you want to change it?
   A: _____

2. **A:** My husband (*wife*) and I have only one car. Can I please change my work schedule?
   B: No, I'm sorry. You can't
   A: _____

3. **A:** Can I please take my vacation June 12-16?
   B: I'm sorry, two people are on vacation in June already. Can you take your vacation in May?
   A: _____

4. **A:** My father is very sick. Can I please take tomorrow off?
   B: I'm sorry to hear that. Tomorrow is fine, but I can't pay you.
   A: _____

> - How do you feel when your supervisor says no to you?
> - What do you do when this happens?

What Should They Do?

Circle the best answer or write your own answer.

1. Juan's supervisor asks him to work early the next day. Juan says yes, but then he forgets. When he comes to work, his supervisor is angry. What should Juan do?
    a. He should quit his job.
    b. He should apologize.
    c. He should say it wasn't his fault.
    d. _____

2. Aruna is driving home from her vacation in another state. Her car breaks down. She knows she will miss a day or more of work. What should she do?
    a. Nothing. She doesn't think her supervisor will know.
    b. She should wait to call until she knows when she can come to work.
    c. She should call work as soon as she can.
    d. _____

3. Juan and Paola are scheduled to work together today. Juan did not come to work, and he did not call. What should Paola do?
    a. Nothing. Juan probably has a good reason.
    b. She should be angry. Now she has too much work.
    c. She should ask her supervisor to call Juan. Maybe he is in trouble.
    d. _____

4. Sam wants to quit his job in four weeks. What should he do?
    a. He should tell his supervisor right away.
    b. He should tell his supervisor in two weeks.
    c. He should say nothing because he thinks his supervisor will be angry.
    d. _____

Chapter 15
Moving Ahead

I KNOW THERE'S A POSITION OPEN

Look and Listen

Mohammad: You know, Sarah is leaving next week.

Mr. Connors: And you're interested in her job?

Mohammad: Yes. I think I would be a good waiter.

Mr. Connors: Why do you think so?

Mohammad: I was a waiter in another restaurant. And Rosa showed me how she works here.

Mr. Connors: Your English has improved since you started.

Mohammad: Thank you. I enjoy talking to customers.

Mr. Connors: You're a good worker, Mohammad. I'll see what I can do.

Check Your Understanding
Circle Yes or No.

1. There's a waiter's position open.   Yes   No
2. Mohammad is a waiter now.   Yes   No
3. Mohammad has worked as a waiter before.   Yes   No
4. Mohammad's English is better now.   Yes   No
5. Mohammad likes to talk to customers.   Yes   No
6. Mohammad gets the job right away.   Yes   No

Practice
Speak to 3 students. Complete the chart.

	Student 1	Student 2	Student 3
Name			
How long have you been at your present job?			
Have you worked anywhere else?			
How long have you been taking English classes?			

YOU SAID I COULD GET A RAISE

Look and Listen

Tomás: Good morning, Mr. Connors. I came in early because I wanted to talk to you. Do you have time?

Mr. Connors: Sure. How can I help you?

Tomás: I started working here more than a year ago. You said I could get a raise after one year.

Mr. Connors: Has it been a year already? I'm sorry.

Tomás: I often work overtime and I'm never out sick.

Mr. Connors: And you do excellent work.

Tomás: Thanks.

Mr. Connors: I think you deserve a raise. Let me think about how much. I'll tell you in a few days.

Tomas: Thank you, Mr. Connors. I appreciate it.

Practice

Circle the letter of the answer you think is best.

1. Lemma wants to apply for a better position in the same restaurant. What should he say to his supervisor?
   a. Talk about how much he needs the job
   b. Ask for the job
   c. Talk about how well he has done in his present job and then ask for the better position

2. Kareem wants a raise. What should he say to his supervisor?
   a. Ask for a raise
   b. Talk about how well he has done, then ask for a raise
   c. Talk about how much he needs a raise because he now has his own apartment

3. Mohammad doesn't get the waiter's position he wants. What should he do?
   a. Ask his supervisor what he can do to get ready for future jobs and look for other opportunities
   b. Get angry at his supervisor
   c. Say nothing, but look for other opportunities

4. Joe's supervisor said he could get a raise after one year. Now it's more than a year, so he asks for a raise. His supervisor says OK. Joe waits a month, but he gets no raise. What should Joe do?
   a. Wait one more week to talk to his supervisor again
   b. Go back to his supervisor now and explain the problem
   c. Ask another supervisor for the raise

5. Rosa thinks she deserves a raise, but she is afraid her English isn't good enough to talk to her supervisor. What should she do?
   a. Wait until she feels confident with her English
   b. Talk to another supervisor who speaks her language
   c. Try to talk to her supervisor in English

- At your job, do you get a raise each year?
- What do you say when you ask for a raise?
- Do you have a union contract?

VOCABULARY

Match the picture with the correct word. Then add another word.

> on time   organized
> friendly   clean

1. _____

2. _____

3. _____

4. _____

TALKING TOGETHER

Look at the employee record.

```
                        Employee Record
Name: Shaheen, Mohammad           Comments:
Address: 444 Main St.             often works late
         Redwood City, CA 94063   late to work 2/10, 2/28
Phone: 368-2145                   works well with staff
S.S. Number: 565-82-4163          makes sure job is done
Starting Date: 1/20/91            sometimes forgets time
Position: Busboy                     sheet and paperwork
                                  works quickly
                                  works well under pressure
```

1. Talk to another student about Mohammad.

    A: What does Mohammad do well?

    B: He _____.

    He _____.

    He _____.

    He _____.

    He _____.

2. Now have a conversation with your supervisor. You may use the words in the box below to help you.

    Supervisor: What do you do well?

    You: I _____.

    I _____.

    I _____.

    I _____.

    I _____.

```
finish my work on time    smile at customers
dress neatly              know my job
can talk to people well   do what my boss tells me
get to work on time       keep my work area neat
```

one hundred seventy-five 175

WORDS FOR WORK

Fill in the blanks with the words from the box.

> raise   interested
> promotion   deserve
> customers   improved

Rosa: You know, Sarah is leaving this week. Are you _____ in her job?

Mohammad: I don't know. I think I could be a good waiter. My English has _____ since I started.

Rosa: And the _____ like you, Mohammad.

Mohammad: Thanks, Rosa. Maybe I will ask for that _____.

Rosa: You _____ it!

Mohammad: Maybe Mr. Connors will give me a _____, too.

SPEAKING PRACTICE

Practice the following conversations with a partner. In the second conversation, use the words from the box to fill in the blanks. Then practice using information from your own job.

cook	clean kitchen equipment
waiter	take orders
busboy	mop floors
waitress	serve water
dishwasher	clean tables
cook American food	set tables
carry heavy trays	write up bills

1. **A:** I'm interested in a waiter's position.
   B: What kind of work are you doing now?
   A: I'm a cafeteria attendant.
   B: What are you good at on your job?
   A: I know how much food to serve. I can carry a full tray of dishes. And I enjoy talking to customers.
   B: Do you think you can take food orders?
   A: Yes, I'm sure I can learn.

2. **A:** I'm interested in a _____'s position.
   B: What kind of work are you doing now?
   A: I'm a _____.
   B: What are you good at on your job?
   A: I _____. I _____. And I _____.
   B: Do you think you can _____?
   A: Yes, I'm sure I can learn.

SPEAKING PRACTICE

Part 1

Speak to three students. Complete the following chart.

What's your name?			
What's your job now?			
What are you good at on your job?	1. 2. 3.	1. 2. 3.	1. 2. 3.
What kind of new job do you want?			
What do you need to learn for this new job?			

Part 2

With one or two other students, think of more questions a supervisor might ask you. Then write possible answers.

Example: 1. Question: Have you done this kind of work before?
Answer: No, but I know I can learn the job.
2. Question: Are you strong enough for the job?
Answer: Yes, I did a lot of lifting on my last job.

Question: _____?
Answer: _____.
Question: _____?
Answer: _____.
Question: _____?
Answer: _____.

STRUCTURE WORK

Choose the past tense of the word below the blank.

Example: The supervisor ___raised___ Rosa's salary.
_{raise}

1. Mr. Connors _____ what he could do for Tomás.
   _{ask}

2. He _____ at the applicant's employee record.
   _{look}

3. Tomás _____ a raise.
   _{want}

4. Mohammad's English had _____ since he started work.
   _{improve}

5. Mohammad _____ at his job for eight months. Then he asked
   _{work}
   for a promotion.

6. Tomás _____ his job more than a year ago.
   _{start}

7. The busboy _____ all the tables. Then he swept the floor.
   _{clean}

8. Tomás _____ American food at his last job.
   _{cook}

9. Tomás _____ all the orders from the customers and he didn't
   _{take}
   make any mistakes.

10. Mohammad _____ the floor before the restaurant opened.
    _{mop}

PROBLEM SOLVING

What Do You Say?

Circle the letter of the answer you think is best.

1. Your supervisor asks you if you can learn a new job. You think you can. What do you say?
   a. "Yes, I'm sure I can."
   b. "Well, I think I can."
   c. "I can try."

2. You tell your supervisor you want a raise. He asks you why. What do you say?
   a. "The landlord raised my rent."
   b. "I do my job better now."
   c. "I've been here for six months."

3. You ask your supervisor for a promotion. She asks you why you want it. What do you say?
   a. "I don't like the person who works with me now."
   b. "I'm tired of my job and I want to do something different."
   c. "I've watched the other workers. I know I can do it."

4. You ask your supervisor for a raise. He says no. What do you do?
   a. Ask your supervisor what work you need to do to get a raise in the future.
   b. Say nothing.
   c. Tell your supervisor you're upset.

5. You ask your supervisor for a promotion. She says you can try for another job which is not higher. You don't want that job. What do you do?
   a. Try for the job you don't want.
   b. Answer, "No, thank you," for the job you don't want.
   c. Tell her you think you can do the job you want.

Talk About Your Strengths

With a partner, act out the following conversations. Practice both parts.

1. **A:** What can you do well on your job?
   B: _____

2. **A:** I want to move up to a _____'s position because my English is pretty good now.
   B: Tell me why you think you can do the job.
   A: _____

3. **A:** I want to move up to a manager's position because I've been here for two years now.
   B: I think you need more than two years of experience here to be a manager.
   A: _____

4. **A:** I think I deserve a raise. I've been here for one year.
   B: Tell how your work has improved.
   A: _____

- In your country, is it OK to tell your supervisor you're good at your job?
- Do you sometimes feel you need to tell people that you do good work?

JAN 1 7 2001